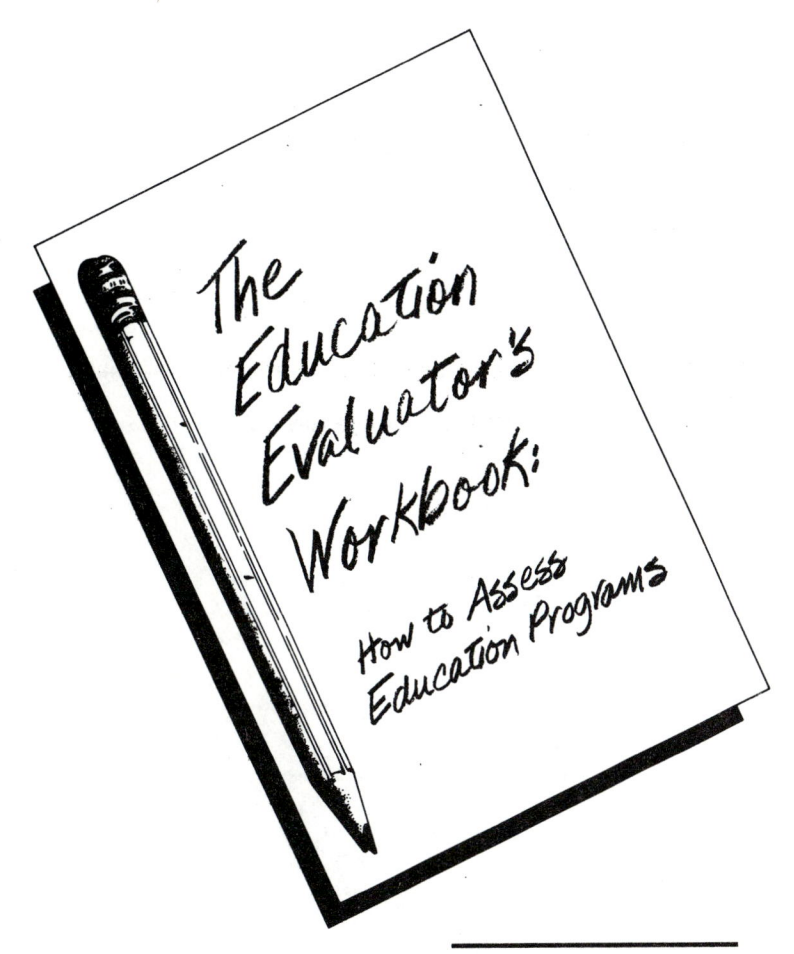

The Education Evaluator's Workbook: How to Assess Education Programs

Leslie A. Ratzlaff, Editor

Education Research Group
Capitol Publications, Inc.
1101 King Street
Alexandria, Virginia 22314

Also published by the Education Research Group:

The Child Abuse Crisis: Impact on the Schools
P.L. 94-142: Impact on the Schools
AIDS: Impact on the Schools
Education Directory: A Guide to Decision-Makers in the Federal Government, the States and
 Education Associations
Inside the Education Department: An Office-by-Office Review
Education Regulations Library

Copyright © 1986 by the Education Research Group,
Capitol Publications, Inc.
Marcy Swerdlin, Publisher
Roberta Weiner, Executive Editor

All Rights Reserved. No part of this book may be reproduced or used in any form without permission in writing from the publisher. Address inquiries to: Permissions Editor, Education Research Group, Capitol Publications, 1101 King St., Alexandria, Va. 22314, (703)683-4100.

Printed in the United States of America.

Cover design by Linda C. McDonald. Interior design and production by Rosette Graham, Les Black Carr and Aden Hachman.

INTRODUCTION

The Education Evaluator's Workbook is a compilation of ideas and methods that work. Culled from the Education Research Group's monthly newsletter, *How to Evaluate Education Programs*, the lessons reprinted in this volume take you from before the evaluation to data collection to surveys and statistics.

Included are 15 lessons in eight categories, gathered in a format you can use as a workbook. We have reprinted blank forms from the lessons so you can tear them out and use in them in your own evaluations. We have left blank pages for you to jot down notes. And we have collected formulas commonly used for evaluation at the end of this volume for easy reference.

The lessons in this volume were written by Arlene Fink and Jacqueline Kosecoff, education evaluators who run Fink & Kosecoff Inc., a research and development firm in Santa Monica, Calif. Each has broad experience in conducting evaluations and training evaluators for education and health programs.

The authors have conducted evaluations for the former National Institute of Education, the University of Southern California Medical Center, the National Science Foundation, the U.S. Department of Education, the RAND Corp. and the American Institutes for Research.

We hope you find this and other volumes of *The Education Evaluator's Workbook* tools you can use in your job or in the classroom.

Roberta Weiner
Executive Editor
Education Research Group

TABLE OF CONTENTS

INTRODUCTION i

PART ONE—BEFORE THE EVALUATION
Lesson 1: How To Conduct An Evaluability Assessment 1
Lesson 2: How To Pretest Evaluation Reports And Materials 13

PART TWO—DATA COLLECTION AND ANALYSIS
Lesson 3: How To Analyze Categorical And Continuous Data 23
Lesson 4: How To Train Data Collectors 33

PART THREE—SURVEYS
Lesson 5: How To Choose A Survey Design 41
Lesson 6: How to Conduct A Survey 51

PART FOUR—STATISTICS
Lesson 7: How To Use The Normal Curve 61
Lesson 8: How To Weigh Statistical Significance 71

PART FIVE—COMPARISON
Lesson 9: How To Compare Programs And Participants 77
Lesson 10: How To Use Pattern Analysis 87

PART SIX—EVALUATING TEACHERS
Lesson 11: How To Measure Teaching Performance 95
Lesson 12: How To Use A Nominal Group Process To Define Merit 107

PART SEVEN—COST
Lesson 13: How To Evaluate On A Shoestring 115
Lesson 14: How To Calculate The Costs Of Evaluation 121

PART EIGHT—PROBLEMS OF EVALUATION
Lesson 15: How to Avoid Common Evaluation Hazards 133

EVALUATION FORMULAS 143

Lesson 1

How To Conduct An Evaluability Assessment

Evaluability assessment is one way to find out whether a program, or parts of a program, are "ready" to be evaluated. Evaluation is not likely to lead to improvement in program performance unless program objectives are well defined, activities show some signs of making progress toward those objectives, and the people in charge of the program know how they will use the evaluation information.

Evaluation assessment can make an evaluation easier to manage by pinpointing the parts of a program that justify the evaluator's time and expense. The following steps to follow in conducting an evaluability assessment are adapted from Evaluation: Promise and Performance, by Joseph S. Wholey.

Step 1: Define The Program To Be Evaluated

What does the program consist of? What is its purpose? Can you explain which activities are part of the program you will evaluate and which ones are not? In evaluating curriculum, for example, one school district might decide to evaluate its entire fourth-grade language arts program, while another may only evaluate certain parts, such as composition or spelling.

Step 2: Collect Information On The Intended Program

Next, the evaluator describes program activities, objectives, causal assumptions and measures of program performance, by drawing on information from program documents such as committee reports, research reports, program memoranda, speeches, documents describing organization and staffing, grant applications and reports from the field. Don't rely entirely on documents and records, however. Be sure to spend enough time with those in charge of the program to understand their goals and expectations.

To get the information you need, you might conduct interviews or "user surveys" with those in charge of the program. This will help you clarify: (a) who will be the primary users of the evaluation information and for what purposes; (b) how the primary users define the program and its objectives; (c) whether there is any disagreement over appropriate measures of program performance; and (d) how satisfied the users are with prior evaluations and with the information they are currently receiving.

If possible, take notes or tapes of the interviews so you can state objectives and measures of program performance in their own words.

Step 3: Synthesize Information For A Clear Picture Of The Program

The next step is to synthesize the information obtained from documents and user surveys in a form that makes clear the logic of the program. Some people do this by developing a flow diagram or "logic model" that graphically represents intended source inputs, activities, outcomes (including important side effects), and assumed casual relationships. If management has a different view of the program from those at higher policy levels, you may have to construct different logic models.

Another way to synthesize the information you have is to use the "evaluator's program description." This displays goals and activities, accompanied by a statement of expectations called 'evidence of program merit." The advantage of this format is that it brings to light some of the conflicts and redundancies that exist in the program. You can circulate the document to managers as well as policymakers, and then use consensus techniques, such as Delphi, to clear up any confusion.

Goals	Activities	Evidence of Program Merit
1. To encourage students to take more responsibility for their own health.	Introduce new health curriculum materials that emphasize prevention.	Special curriculum materials are distributed and used in the classroom.
	Classroom presentations on diet, exercise and health by local cardiologist and college football star.	Discussions on diet, exercise, smoking, etc., are led by respected doctors and athletes.
		Students demonstrate significantly more understanding of the importance of diet and exercise than they did at the beginning of the school year and more than comparable students who did not participate in the program.
2. etc.	etc.	etc.

Step 4: Decide How To Measure Program Performance

Here you must make sure that each part of the program you are evaluating has specific performance standards and that you can collect performance information that others will believe. You may have to explain the different methods generally used for collecting data and how much they cost, so that sponsors can decide whether they prefer interviews, questionnaires, observations, record reviews, paper and pencil tests, etc.

Step 5: Collect Information On Program Reality

Now you must examine the actual program in operation. This will give you a chance to assess the plausibility of program assumptions and the feasibility of measuring program performance.

One reason costly evaluations sometimes produce inconclusive findings is because the actual program in the field is often very different from the program that exists in the minds of the evaluator and the sponsor. Another reason is that some programs operate in a way that makes it impossible to detect program effects. Still another is because the necessary data can't be obtained. Always study program operations and data availability before you choose your evaluation design.

For a complete picture of the program in operation, make site visits to find out what activities are going on, what results are anticipated, and what measurements and comparisons are feasible. At each site you should examine project activity, work plans, reports, etc. Interview the project director, staff members who are responsible for each of the major activities, and those who are responsible for collecting data on project operations.

Now examine all the available evidence to determine which of the program objectives and expectations are plausible. An objective is plausible if there is some likelihood that the program activities will lead toward the objective. Objectives may be implausible for many different reasons. Some of these might be that the program lacks necessary resources, has unrealistic schedules, isn't carrying out the planned activities, or simply lacks a rationale for choosing the particular activities to accomplish program objectives. Classify each objective as plausible or implausible.

Step 6: Study Program Reality To Determine Plausibility Of Objectives

Now put the information obtained from program documents and site visits into a form that depicts the activities under way, actual and anticipated results of those activities, and possible sources of data on activities and results. Two important questions are answered:

- ▶ What data can I get on program performance?
- ▶ Does the real program have some likelihood of reaching management's goals and expectations?

Use your knowledge of field operations to draw up a flow model representing: (1) actual program inputs, activities and outcomes; and (2) the points at which you can measure them. Such models are sometimes called "equivalency models," since they are supposed to be equivalent to field operations.

Step 7: Identify The Options

Now you have all you need to decide what part or parts of the program are ready for evaluation. Wholey defines the <u>evaluable program</u> as "the portion of the program for which those in charge have defined plausible, measurable objectives; for which there are feasible sources of performance data; and for which likely uses of program performance information have been defined."

Draw up an <u>evaluable model</u> of the program, eliminating all implausible objectives and all data collection that is not likely to be used by program management.

You also should be able to identify alternative evaluable models or "evaluation/management options." Each option includes a set of plausible objectives, performance measurements, comparisons to be made, and possible management uses of the resulting information. Feel free to suggest objectives and performance measures that appear feasible, considering existing data and possible new data sources.

Step 8: Present The Assessment To Program Managers

The final step in evaluability assessment is to present your work to those in charge of the program so they can verify your findings and decide what to do next. Your presentation should include:

▶ The logic model—an accurate descriptive model of the intended program, based on program documents and user surveys, <u>or</u>

An Evaluator's Program Description with the goals, activities, and anticipated evidence of program success;

▶ The equivalency model—a model that describes what is actually happening in the program (its inputs, activities and outcomes) and indicates where and how data can be obtained on program performance;

▶ The evaluable model—your assessment of the program that can usefully be evaluated, based on current activities and given the feasibility of measuring progress toward plausible objectives;

▶ An explanation of how you arrived at the evaluable model;

▶ A description of the program performance information that could be collected;

▶ Suggestions for ways to use the evaluation information; and

▶ One or more alternative evaluable models—options that are feasible if management if willing to modify program activities or objectives, or to collect and use new data on program performance.

Is Evaluability Assessment Really Something New?

Nick L. Smith of the Northwest Regional Educational Laboratory says the same idea has been around for a while in what has been called the causal-modeling approach to evaluation. After reading a book on evaluability by Leonard Rutman and reflecting on his own experience conducting a pre-evaluation assessment, Smith writes:

> "One of the limitations of Rutman's approach is that one would not evaluate any program or program component which is not 'ready.' This suggests that developmental programs, innovative projects, and those with serious problems requiring immediate corrective feedback are likely to be judged as unready and consequently unfit for evaluation. Thus those programs most in need of evaluation may be the ones least likely to be evaluated ...."

How To Conduct An Evaluability Assessment

Another obvious point about this approach i[s]
about whether to do an evaluation or no[t]
evaluations are required by law, ready
may be many instances where an evaluabi[lity]
uation planning, there are probably s[ome]
evaluator has a real option to perform
results of the evaluability assessment.

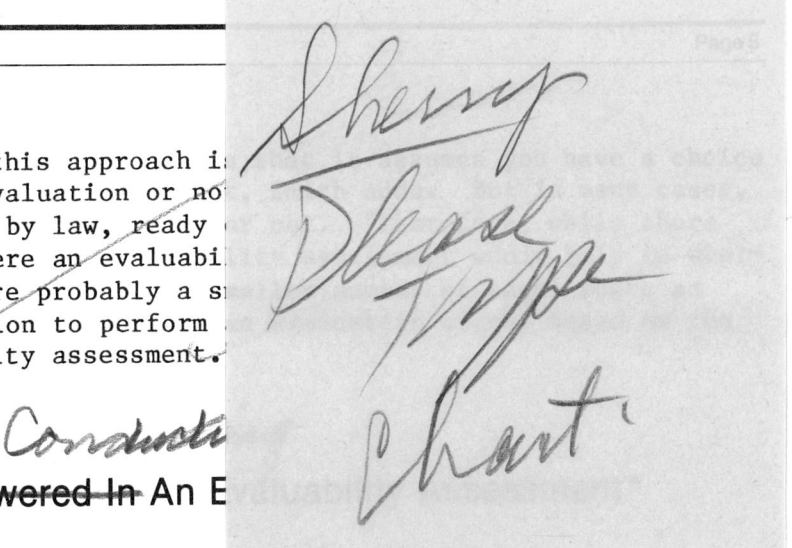

Checklist: ~~Questions Answered In~~ An E[valuability Assessment]*

Evaluability Assessment Step	Questions Answered
Step 1: Selecting the Program to be Evaluated	■ What program activities and objectives are the main focus of the evaluation?
Step 2: Collecting Information on the Intended Program	■ What are management's program objectives and expectations? (What resources, activities, objectives and causal assumptions make up management's intended program?) ■ What are the objectives and expectations of those at other management and policy levels? ■ What measures of program performance have been selected by those in charge of the program?
Step 3: Modeling: Synthesizing Information on the Intended Program	■ What is the logic of causal assumptions that link resource inputs, program activities, outcomes and impacts (from the point of view of the intended users of the evaluation?)
Step 4: Analysis: Identification of User's Measures of Program Performance	■ For which of the anticipated resource inputs, program activities, outcomes and impacts (including important side effects) are there agreed-on measures acceptable to the intended users of the evaluation?
Step 5: Collecting Information on Program Reality	■ What are the actual program inputs, activities and outcomes?
Step 6: Modeling: Synthesizing Information on Program Reality and Analyzing the Plausibility of Program Objectives	■ What data are obtainable on program performance? (Are there data sources for management's agreed-on measures?) ■ Is there a program in place that is likely to achieve management's objectives and expectations for the program?
Step 7: Identification of Evaluation/Management Options	■ What portion of the intended program is ready for useful evaluation? ■ How would management use information on program performance? ■ What evaluation/management options would enhance program performance?
Step 8: Presentation to Management and Mangement Response	■ What are the likely uses of the evaluation information)? What range of actions might the intended user take or consider as a result of various possible findings? ■ What level of confidence would the user require before acting on the information? ■ To what extent is the intended user inclined or able to change program activities or objectives?

*From *Evaluation: Promise and Performance* by Joseph S. Wholey.

References

Fink, A., and J. Kosecoff. *An Evaluation Primer*, Alexandria, Va.: Capitol Publications Inc., 1978.

Rutman, P. *Planning Useful Evaluations: Evaluability Assessment*, Beverly Hills, Calif.: Sage Publications, 1980.

Smith, N.L. "Evaluability Assessment: A Retrospective Illustration and Review." *Educational Evaluation and Policy Analysis*, Vol. 3, No. 1, Washington, D.C.: American Educational Research Association, Jan.-Feb. 1981.

Wholey, J.S. *Evaluation: Promise and Performance*, Washington, D.C.: The Urban Institute, 1979.

This lesson is reprinted from the July 1985 issue of
How To Evaluate Education Programs.

How To Conduct An Evaluability Assessment   Page 7

Here is an extra evaluability assessment checklist for you to cut out and use.

Evaluability Assessment Step	Questions Answered
Step 1: Selecting the Program to be Evaluated	■ What program activities and objectives are the main focus of the evaluation?
Step 2: Collecting Information on the Intended Program	■ What are management's program objectives and expectations? (What resources, activities, objectives and causal assumptions make up management's intended program?) ■ What are the objectives and expectations of those at other management and policy levels? ■ What measures of program performance have been selected by those in charge of the program?

Evaluability Assessment Step	Questions Answered
Step 3: Modeling: Synthesizing Information on the Intended Program	■ What is the logic of causal assumptions that link resource inputs, program activities, outcomes and impacts (from the point of view of the intended users of the evaluation?)
Step 4: Analysis: Identification of User's Measures of Program Performance	■ For which of the anticipated resource inputs, program activities, outcomes and impacts (including important side effects) are there agreed-on measures acceptable to the intended users of the evaluation?

Evaluability Assessment Step	Questions Answered
Step 5: Collecting Information on Program Reality	■ What are the actual program inputs, activities and outcomes?
Step 6: Modeling: Synthesizing Information on Program Reality and Analyzing the Plausibility of Program Objectives	■ What data are obtainable on program performance? (Are there data sources for management's agreed-on measures?) ■ Is there a program in place that is likely to achieve management's objectives and expectations for the program?

Evaluability Assessment Step	Questions Answered
Step 7: Identification of Evaluation/Management Options	■ What portion of the intended program is ready for useful evaluation? ■ How would management use information on program performance? ■ What evaluation/management options would enhance program performance?
Step 8: Presentation to Management and Mangement Response	■ What are the likely uses of the evaluation information)? What range of actions might the intended user take or consider as a result of various possible findings? ■ What level of confidence would the user require before acting on the information? ■ To what extent is the intended user inclined or able to change program activities or objectives?

NOTES

Lesson 2

How To Pretest Evaluation Reports And Materials

What do these evaluators have in common?

▶ Evaluator A is at a meeting with the board of education to persuade the members to evaluate a new language arts curriculum before adopting it. The purchase of certain books and films is at stake.

▶ Evaluator B is explaining to the parents association about a recent evaluation of the health curriculum, outlining the objectives and methods of the study and comparing the results for students in the experimental and control groups.

▶ Evaluator C has submitted a report to the superintendent about the district's science program, describing the courses and materials that were most effective in reaching their objectives and presenting data to show the areas still needing improvement.

All three of these evaluators are engaging in one of their most important jobs: communicating with policymakers and the public. Before an evaluation begins, they must be sure the chief participants understand why it is needed and what questions it is expected to answer. When an evaluation is under way, they must make progress reports. When it is completed, they must analyze the results and explain them to others.

Telling others about evaluation is often difficult. Its technical nature makes it hard to translate into every language, and since most evaluations don't produce unequivocal results ("This is the best program for every student,") the information gleaned from evaluation may be ambiguous or inconclusive. The absence of clear-cut findings is hard to explain.

Communicating negative or controversial results is another problem. How can you break the bad news or explain unexpected results without having them misinterpreted? Getting your message across accurately and clearly is an important part of your job. To be sure you're doing it right, try pretesting your message.

The following ideas are suggested in a booklet from the National Cancer Institute, Pretesting In Health Communications: Methods, Examples and Resources for Improving Health Messages and Materials. You can use them in evaluating education programs and particularly in reporting the results of evaluation studies.

What Is Pretesting And What Does It Measure?

Pretesting, or field-testing, is one type of formative evaluation. The term is used to describe a process for getting reaction to messages and materials before they become final.

One of the things pretesting can tell you is whether one format is better than another for reaching the target audience. Are short summaries better than detailed reports? Are newspapers better than radio? Are letters better than brochures?

Pretesting also can tip you off to trouble spots, perhaps revealing that the wording of your message or report is too difficult for your target audience.

Design your pretest to find out whether your message:

- Attracts and holds the audience's attention;
- Clearly conveys your main ideas;
- Seems important to those you want to reach;
- Is believed and accepted.

Six Steps For Planning And Improving Your Message

The Office of Cancer Communications has devised a six-step process for planning and improving information campaigns aimed at cancer patients or the general public. The last step feeds back into the first, so new ideas and information can be used to make the next effort even better. You can use the same system in your work with education evaluation.

Here's how the National Cancer Institute pictures the process:

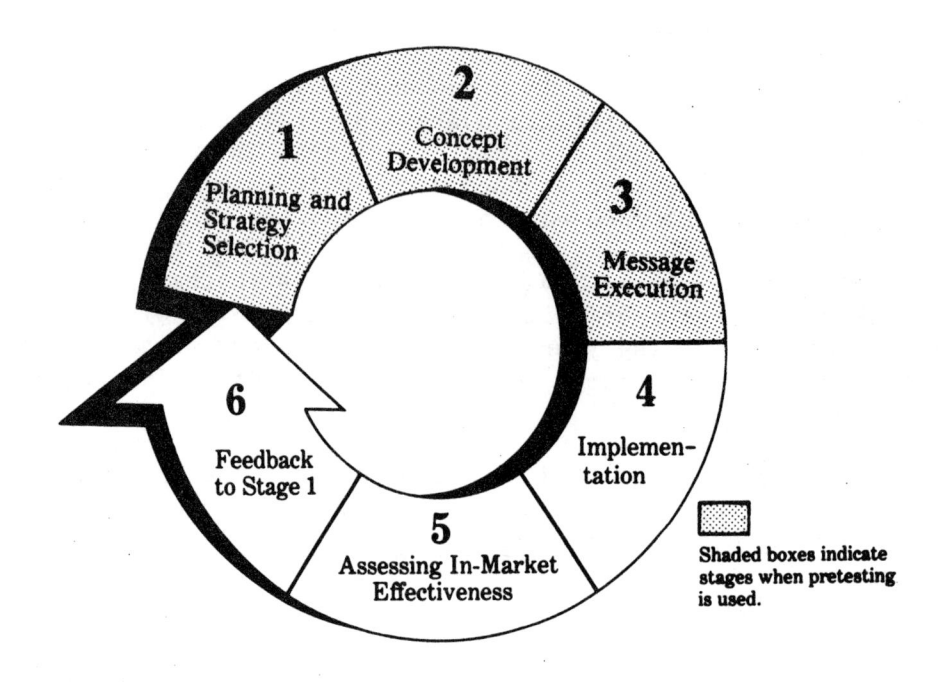

1. Planning and Strategy Selection
2. Concept Development
3. Message Execution
4. Implementation
5. Assessing In-Market Effectiveness
6. Feedback to Stage 1

Shaded boxes indicate stages when pretesting is used.

Step 1: Planning And Strategy Selection

To begin with, try to anticipate what your audience needs to know. How much do they understand about the program? About this evaluation? Is one group particularly critical of the program or hostile to your evaluation? Will people read reports or would they rather hear you explain your findings?

If you're not sure how your target audience feels about certain issues, see if you can find public surveys or minutes of community meetings that covered those topics. In some cases, you might want to conduct surveys or interviews yourself. The main purpose of this stage is to help you discover what your audience needs to know and to begin thinking about how to get the message to them.

Draw up a strategy statement. It should include your objectives, the target audiences you want to reach and a summary of the information you want to communicate.

Step 2: Developing Concepts

Concepts are not finished messages, just rough ideas about how to get your message across. Choose several different approaches and try each one on at least two or three people who are typical of your audience.

When the National Cancer Institute tested four different posters for a campaign to acquaint the public with the dangers of exposure to asbestos, they found that men didn't pay much attention to the message when it was presented by a doctor. More successful versions used an elderly shipyard worker and a movie celebrity of World War II vintage. Discoveries such as this save time and money later.

When you pretest rough concepts, listen to the language used by people from your target sample. Try using some of their vernacular to make your material easier to understand. Avoid evaluation jargon, especially terms such as quasi-experiment, statistically significant, formative and summative, theoretical framework, and so on. Keep it simple. Even sophisticated audiences don't like jargon.

Step 3: Executing The Message

Once you have selected the concepts that seem most promising, try some complete messages. This is the time to submit draft versions of evaluation summaries, graphics or reports to outsiders for review. You may want to subject your work to a readability test to see what level of reading comprehension it takes to understand it.

Here are examples of what pretesting can do for you at this stage:

- ▶ <u>Assess comprehension</u> -- How well do people understand the message?

- ▶ <u>Assess recall</u> -- How well do people remember the message later? For example, would it help to use boldface type for important findings?

▶ <u>Identify strong and weak points</u> -- One evaluator found that including a sample of a reading test gave people a better idea of what students were expected to do, but scoring instructions were confusing.

▶ <u>Determine the level of personal interest</u> -- People who have a strong personal interest in the program may be able to help you reach others. Why not ask parents to review an evaluation report to see if it accurately describes the goals and activities of the program in which their children participate?

▶ <u>Gauge sensitive or controversial elements</u> -- If the wording or conclusions of your report are going to set off controversy or opposition, it's better to know about it now. Unintentional slights can be corrected, and unpopular results can be explained more tactfully.

Steps 4, 5 and 6: Implementation, Evaluation And Feedback

The last three stages of the system are implementation, assessing effectiveness and feedback. Pretesting is not needed to carry out these steps, but it should begin again with step one after you revise your earlier efforts. What you have learned about effective communication in one evaluation can always help you do a better job the next time.

Methods For Pretesting

Pretesting methods suggested by the National Cancer Institute include several kinds of interviews.

▶ <u>Focus group interviews</u>: "A type of qualitative research in which an experienced moderator leads about eight to 10 respondents through a discussion of a selected topic, allowing them to talk freely and spontaneously."

▶ <u>Individual in-depth interviews</u>: "A form of qualitative research consisting of intensive interviews to find out how people think and what they feel about a given topic."

▶ <u>Central location intercept interviews</u>: "Interviews conducted with respondents who are stopped at a highly trafficked location that is frequented by individuals typical of the desired target audience."

Other pretesting methods include using self-administered questionnaires and interviewing "gate keepers," the intermediary groups that stand between you and your intended audience and control the distribution of materials.

The National Cancer Institute also refers to a now-defunct project, the Health Message Testing Service (HMTS), that provided a standard system for pretesting health public service announcements in radio, television and print. The service itself is no longer available, but the Office of Cancer Communications has a videotape that people can use by plugging the message they want to pretest into the spots available on the tape. Evaluators then can do local pretests using standard HMTS questions and a training manual that's available with the tape.

The following set of core HMTS questions is used to assess communication of the main idea, believability, personal relevance and other target audience reactions. The questions are listed here to help you develop your own pretest questionnaires, and they can be modified by changing the words in parentheses to fit the item you are pretesting.

1. Main Idea Communication/Comprehension
What was the *main idea* this (message) was trying to get across to you?
_____
_____

What does this (message) ask you to do?
_____
_____

What action, if any, is the (message) recommending that people take? (Probe: What other actions?)
_____
_____

In your opinion, was there anything in the (message) that was confusing?
_____
_____

Which of these phrases best describes the (message)?
☐ Easy to understand
☐ Hard to understand

2. Likes/Dislikes
In your opinion, was there anything in particular that was worth remembering about the (message)?
_____
_____

What, if anything, did you particularly like about the (message)?
_____
_____

Was there anything in the (message) that you particularly disliked or that bothered you? If yes, what?
_____
_____

3. Believability
In your opinion, was there anything in the (message) that was hard to believe? If yes, what?
_____
_____

Which of these words or phrases best describes how you feel about the (message)?
☐ Believable
☐ Not believable

4. Personal Relevance/Interest
In your opinion, what type of person was this (message) talking to?
Was it talking to ...
☐ Someone like me
☐ Someone else, not me

Was it talking to ...
☐ All people
☐ All people, but especially (the target audience)
☐ Only (the target audience)

Which of these words or phrases best describes how you feel about the (message)?
- ☐ Interesting
- ☐ Not interesting
- ☐ Informative
- ☐ Not informative

Did you learn anything new about (the subject) from this (message)? If yes, what?
_____
_____

5. Other Target Audience Reactions

Target audience reactions to pretest materials can be assessed using pairs of words or phrases or using a 5-point scale. The following is an example of how this is done.

Listed on this sheet of paper are several pairs of words or phrases with the numbers 1 to 5 between them. I'd like you to indicate which number best describes how you feel about the (message). The higher the number, the more you think the phrase on the right describes it. The lower the number, the more you think the phrase on the left describes it. You could also pick any number in between. Now let's go through each set of words. Please tell me which number best describes your reaction to the (message).

Practical	1	2	3	4	5	Not Practical
Too Short	1	2	3	4	5	Too Long
Discouraging	1	2	3	4	5	Encouraging
Comforting	1	2	3	4	5	Alarming
Well Done	1	2	3	4	5	Poorly Done
Not Informative	1	2	3	4	5	Informative

6. For Assessing Artwork

Just looking at the drawing (or picture), what do you think it says?
_____
_____

Is there anything in this drawing (or picture) that would bother or offend people you know?
_____
_____

References

Pretesting in Health Communications: Methods, Examples, and Resources for Improving Health Messages and Materials. National Cancer Institute, Publication Number 84-1493. Bethesda, Md.: 1984.

"Pretesting TV PSAs." National Cancer Institute. Bethesda, Md.

This lesson is reprinted from the September 1985 issue of How To Evaluate Education Programs.

Here is an extra pretest questionnaire sample for you to cut out and use.

1. Main Idea Communication/Comprehension
What was the *main idea* this (message) was trying to get across to you?

_____
_____
_____
_____

What does this (message) ask you to do?

_____
_____
_____
_____

What action, if any, is the (message) recommending that people take? (Probe: What other actions?)

_____
_____
_____
_____

In your opinion, was there anything in the (message) that was confusing?

_____
_____
_____
_____

Which of these phrases best describes the (message)?
☐ Easy to understand
☐ Hard to understand

2. Likes/Dislikes
In your opinion, was there anything in particular that was worth remembering about the (message)?

_____
_____
_____
_____

What, if anything, did you particularly like about the (message)?

_____
_____
_____
_____

Was there anything in the (message) that you particularly disliked or that bothered you? If yes, what?

_____
_____
_____
_____

3. Believability
In your opinion, was there anything in the (message) that was hard to believe? If yes, what?

_____
_____
_____
_____

Which of these words or phrases best describes how you feel about the (message)?
☐ Believable
☐ Not believable

4. Personal Relevance/Interest
In your opinion, what type of person was this (message) talking to?
Was it talking to ...
☐ Someone like me
☐ Someone else, not me

Was it talking to ...
☐ All people
☐ All people, but especially (the target audience)
☐ Only (the target audience)

Which of these words or phrases best describes how you feel about the (message)?
☐ Interesting
☐ Not interesting
☐ Informative
☐ Not informative

Did you learn anything new about (the subject) from this (message)? If yes, what?

_____
_____
_____
_____

5. Other Target Audience Reactions
Target audience reactions to pretest materials can be assessed using pairs of words or phrases or using a 5-point scale. The following is an example of how this is done.

Listed on this sheet of paper are several pairs of words or phrases with the numbers 1 to 5 between them. I'd like you to indicate which number best describes how you feel about the (message). The higher the number, the more you think the phrase on the right describes it. The lower the number, the more you think the phrase on the left describes it. You could also pick any number in between. Now let's go through each set of words. Please tell me which number best describes your reaction to the (message).

Practical	1	2	3	4	5	Not Practical
Too Short	1	2	3	4	5	Too Long
Discouraging	1	2	3	4	5	Encouraging
Comforting	1	2	3	4	5	Alarming
Well Done	1	2	3	4	5	Poorly Done
Not Informative	1	2	3	4	5	Informative

6. For Assessing Artwork
Just looking at the drawing (or picture), what do you think it says?

_____
_____
_____
_____

Is there anything in this drawing (or picture) that would bother or offend people you know?

_____
_____
_____
_____

NOTES

Lesson 3

How To Analyze Categorical And Continuous Data

A school district in California asked an evaluator to find out if the nation's top 10 colleges were accepting the same proportion of students from Monroe High School as from Hart Township. The evaluator's design looked like this:

College	High School	
	Monroe High	Hart Township
1		
2		
3		
4		
5		
6		
7		
8		
9		
10		

Another evaluator in California had to find out if the proportion of state college preparatory program students being accepted by the best colleges was similar to the national average. The evaluator's study design looked like this:

	Colleges									
	1	2	3	4	5	6	7	8	9	10
Frequencies in California										
Frequencies in Nation										

Both evaluators were working with categorical data (in this case, distribution across different colleges) as opposed to continuous, or hierarchical, data (for example, ranking the schools accepting students on a scale from 1 to 100). Variables arranged in classes that can be distinguished from one

23

another but that cannot be arranged into a hierarchy produce categorical information. For example, classifying sex as male or female or program satisfaction as high or low will produce categorical data.

The first part of this month's issue deals with analyzing categorical data; the second part contains some general tips for working with both categorical and continuous data.

Chi Square

The chi square statistic is used to analyze categorical information. Evaluation data often call for two specific procedures that use the chi square statistic: goodness-of-fit testing and contingency table analysis.

Goodness Of Fit

Goodness-of-fit testing is a way of comparing empirically derived data (expressed as frequencies) with theoretically expected results. For example, one evaluation question that would be answered using goodness-of-fit testing would be:

How do participants' approval ratings of Program X compare with the one-third disapproval rate of previous years?

Suppose a new demographic theory predicts a certain population will contain four ethnic groups in the proportions 9:3:3:1, and a random sample of 240 persons resulted in 120, 40, 55 and 25 people in the four categories. You can use a goodness-of-fit test to compare the theoretically expected data with the empirically observed data. The result of the test would be a chi square statistic, which could be computed with the following table and formula:

	Category 1	Category 2	....	Category n
Empirical Frequencies	o_1	o_2	....	o_n
Theoretical Frequencies	t_1	t_2	....	t_n

Chi square formula: $$X^2 = \sum_{i=1}^{n} \frac{(o_i - t_i)^2}{t_i}$$

where:

n = number of categories

o_i = obtained or empirical frequency for the ith category

t_i = theoretical or expected frequency for the ith category

If the obtained or empirical data (o_i) are the same as the theoretical data (t), the fit will be perfect, and the difference ($o_i - t_i$) for each category will be zero, and so will the chi square value. Consequently, the smaller the chi square value, the better the fit; the larger the chi square value, the poorer the fit. You can compare your chi square values with values in chi square tables and accept or reject the goodness of fit at the desired level of statistical significance.

Contingency Tables

Contingency tables are used in chi square analyses to compare two sets of empirical data expressed as frequencies--for example, in testing for a significant relationship between two variables. The relationship between the proportion of students on probation and the students' sex might be organized in a contingency table as follows:

	Not on Probation	On Probation
Male	Number of Observations	Number of Observations
Female	Number of Observations	Number of Observations

You could also use contingency tables to find out if two sets of empirical data are alike--or, in statistical language, whether the two sets are random samples from the same population. For example, you could use a contingency table and a chi square statistic to compare the number of children contracting polio in samples of vaccinated and unvaccinated children:

	Not Vaccinated	Vaccinated
Polio	Number of Observations	Number of Observations
No Polio	Number of Observations	Number of Observations

The chi square statistic used for contingency tables is similar to the one used for goodness-of-fit tests. However, in this case you compare the observed frequencies with expected rather than theoretical frequencies.

EXAMPLE: Chi Square Analysis

The LEGAL program is designed to help students pass law school entrance examinations by giving them practice answering typical standardized examination questions. The school board will approve the LEGAL program if a significantly greater number of LEGAL as opposed to non-LEGAL graduates get accepted by law schools. The evaluation question was, "Is there a statistically significant difference in the rate of law school acceptance between LEGAL graduates and other students?"

The evaluators used a comparison group design. They organized the data into a contingency table with two variables: program participation and admittance to law school.

The evaluators randomly selected 210 college seniors to take part in the evaluation from all the seniors who requested to enroll in LEGAL. The evaluators then randomly accepted half of the 210 students into the program and refused the other half. Two of the refused students were disqualified from the evaluation when they enrolled in another program similar to LEGAL.

Evaluation Sample

No LEGAL	LEGAL
103	105

The evaluators organized the data into a contingency table and used a chi square statistic to test the hypothesis that law school acceptance rates were the same.

	No LEGAL	LEGAL	Totals
Not Admitted	80	30	110
Admitted	23	75	98
Totals	103	105	208

Chi square value (x^2) = 48.4
Degrees of freedom = 1
Significance = $p < .01$

The results of the chi square analysis refuted the hypothesis. The evaluators concluded that the chi square test value of 48.4 indicated a statistically significant difference between LEGAL and non-LEGAL students, with LEGAL students being accepted by law schools more frequently.

Analyzing Evaluation Information: Some Tips

Analyzing evaluation information includes:

- Pilot testing the information analysis;
- Conducting the analysis;
- Interpreting the results of the analysis; and
- Making recommendations <u>if requested</u>.

Pilot Testing

Information analysis techniques must be pilot tested to find out if they work. If the techniques don't work properly, they must be redesigned. A pilot test should include all the planned information analysis activities and should reveal whether:

- Needed information will be available in manageable form;

- Necessary expert personnel and special equipment such as computers are available; and

- Data reduction procedures are efficient and accurate.

Conducting The Analysis

Once the information analysis techniques have been pilot tested and revised, the evaluator can collect and begin to analyze the information. Sometimes evaluation questions require more than one analysis; other times, further analysis is unnecessary unless warranted by the results. For example, to answer the evaluation question, "Which of the four programs is most effective teaching subject X?" you could use a statistical method such as one-way analysis of variance. You would test the hypothesis that there is no difference in average program effectiveness. If the results confirm the hypothesis, then no further analysis would be called for. If, however, the results disprove the hypothesis, you would need additional analysis to find out which programs are responsible for the differences.

An ordered approach to information analysis is the most efficient, yet evaluators often have the notion that most is best. Be careful—security gained from doing all manner of analyses is often illusory. A desultory approach to information analysis is technically unsound because:

- It increases the probability of finding significant results by chance alone;

- It results in a loss of credibility as the evaluator strays from the plan specifically tailored to answer the evaluation question; and

- It is hopelessly inefficient.

Interpreting Results

Assume that data collection and analysis have gone smoothly. What does the evaluator do with the results?

As an example: An evaluation question asked whether shoppers read price-per-pound information used by a food retailer. A survey questionnaire showed that 40 percent of the shoppers said they did read the information. The evaluator now has to consider the following three questions:

1. Is 40 percent sufficient to prove the program's effectiveness?

2. Were the shoppers who responded representative of all shoppers?

3. Does a positive response (reading the price-per-pound information) mean that the information influenced what the shoppers bought?

These questions are typical of problems underlying many evaluations. The first deals with standards of program merit, the second with design strategy and sampling procedures, and the third with validity of information collection and analysis methods. (The last question also points out the importance of asking the right evaluation question in the first place. Was the evaluation trying to find out whether consumers read the information, or whether they read <u>and acted on</u> the information?) <u>If the evaluation is well organized and carefully thought out in the first place, then the information gathered can be interpreted with a minimum of trouble.</u>

Once you have interpreted the analysis results for each evaluation question, you can look at the analyses collectively to get an idea of the effectiveness of the program as a whole. Such overall interpretation is useful in getting a feel for program dynamics or the relationship between parts of the program.

Interpreting results also involves distinguishing between statistical and programmatic significance. Statistical significance tells you how likely it is an outcome is due to chance; programmatic significance tells you whether an outcome makes a difference in terms of program goals--that is, whether the outcome justifies the time, effort and money spent.

Statistical significance and programmatic significance are analogous to reliability and validity. Like reliability, statistical significance is a measure of precision; like validity, programmatic significance is a measure of efficacy and cogency.

Making Recommendations

Finally, analysis results sometimes point to obvious recommendations as to how to improve or certify the effectiveness of a program. The evaluator, however, is not always expected to make--and the client is never obligated to accept--such recommendations.

For the price-per-pound information evaluation, the evaluator supplied the following recommendations when asked:

> Our analysis of descriptive statistics reveals that shoppers between 20 and 40 years old meet the standards set for reading price-per-pound information, while shoppers between 40 and 60 years old do not. We therefore recommend that you continue to give price-per-pound information in markets serving young communities. We also recommend you give price-per-pound information for products bought primarily by young consumers.

This lesson is reprinted from the November 1984 issue of
How To Evaluate Education Programs.

NOTES

Lesson 4

How To Train Data Collectors

Evaluations have the most influence when they're timely and use the best information around. But information collection can be complicated. Sometimes it pays to train people to get the information you need when you need it, using the methods you have chosen.

Three rules to remember when training:

- Pay attention to detail
- Standardize
- Anticipate

Getting Together: The Time And The Place

Whether you are training two data collectors or 20, it is important to find a time when all of you can get together. The advantage of meeting is that everyone can develop a standard vocabulary and share problems.

If you rely on outside data collectors, this will probably mean meeting before or after regular working hours. If you want to train school counselors to complete a new student progress record, for example, you might have to schedule your training session late in the afternoon. A training session for parents would probably have to wait until evening, since many of them will be working during the day.

If the trainees have to travel to reach you, you must think about paying for gasoline or other means of private or public transportation.

Once there, trainees must have enough space to sit and write or perform any activities you will require of them. If you want them to interview one another as practice for their real tasks, be sure the room is large enough so that two or more separate groups won't interfere with each other. You may even need several rooms.

If training takes more than an hour and an half, you should provide some form of refreshments. If you can't afford to do that, at least give trainees time to obtain their own. Be prepared to point out the location of the nearest rest rooms, water fountain, coffee machine, and so on.

Spelling It Out: The Training Manual

Trainees should be taken step-by-step through their tasks and given an opportunity to ask questions. It's also essential to tell them some of the reasons for their tasks, so they can anticipate problems and be prepared to solve them.

The most efficient way to make sure the trainees have all the information they need to perform their jobs is to prepare a manual. Here you can explain what they are to do--and when, where, why and how they are to do it. A three-ring binder makes it easy to add pages if necessary.

What You Are Supposed To Do

In this section of the manual, briefly describe the tasks each data collector will be expected to perform. This short checklist is one example of a list of tasks for data collectors who will be conducting telephone interviews:

- Obtain list of names to call;
- Check to be sure list is readable;
- Count the number of interview forms to see if you have enough;
- Check interview forms for clarity;
- Be sure you have a stamped envelope with our address;
- Make phone calls;
- Complete all forms; and
- Mail forms to us.

Each of these tasks must be fully explained later on, in the "how" section of the manual. That is, you will eventually have to tell how to get the list of names to call, where phone calls are to be made, and what a complete form looks like. The purpose of the checklist is just to give an overview of the steps in the data collector's job.

Why You Are Doing This

In some evaluation studies, data collectors are told very little about the reasons for their tasks. The rationale seems to be that the less they know, the less likely they are to try to answer--on their own--questions that people ask about the evaluation. But many collectors seem to perform better if they understand and feel a part of what they're doing.

The more confident you are that your data collection strategy is reliable, the less you need to tell the data collector about the purpose of the evaluation. If your survey of community attitudes toward educational reforms uses questions developed by one of the big survey research companies, for example, you can expect to get the data you need without much explanation. But suppose you are using teachers to collect data from local doctors for an evaluation of a school health program. Those teachers had better be prepared to answer questions about the evaluation, and probably about the data collection forms.

If you decide to explain what the data collectors are doing, you might want to try a simple question-and-answer format. Suppose, for example, you are evaluating a school-community health program for asthmatic children. You want to find out whether the program has been good for the children. Do they attend school more often? Do they see the doctor less? Do they use less medication?

To answer these questions, you want to use school records for attendance information and medical records for information about visits to the doctor. The school has given its permission but the doctors haven't. Can you get their permission if you promise confidentiality? Are the medical records incomplete or hard to read? Is it worth the expense of making a trip to look at the records when a phone call might do as well?

You decide to test the value of the medical record as a source of information. Here's how you might explain what you're doing to the data collectors, and later to the doctors:

<u>What is the purpose of this study of medical records?</u> We are trying to find out if the medical record is the best source of information about asthmatic children's visits to the doctor and their use of medication.

<u>What is the school/community program for asthmatic children?</u> This program involves N schools, Y doctors and the University Teaching Hospital in a joint effort to help asthmatic children function more independently.

Other questions that help to explain the purpose of the evaluation are:

- ▶ Who's paying for the program? The evaluation?
- ▶ Who's responsible?
- ▶ What's in it for the doctors?
- ▶ How much of their time will it take?
- ▶ How will confidentiality be ensured?

How To Collect The Information

The "how" of data collection is the essence of the data collector's task. Be sure you take trainees through all of the forms, define the terms and give them an opportunity to practice any difficult tasks.

The following telephone survey form, developed by a leading survey research firm (name changed) illustrates the complexity of the material data collectors are sometimes expected to use. Suppose you were training data collectors to complete this form. Here are some of the things you should consider:

- ▶ Ask each trainee to read the questions aloud (beginning with "Hello") to be sure they speak clearly and pronounce the words correctly.

- ▶ Explain how to use the grids. ("Look at the top first and circle the correct number of adults. Then look at the column on the left and circle the correct number of female adults ....")

- ▶ Explain the following terms: "adult designated respondent," "child proxy," "proxy for adult."

S2a. And how many children under the age of 17 in your family live in your apartment or living quarters? Please include any children temporarily in the hospital or any other health or convalescent facility.

IF NONE, RECORD BELOW AND SKIP TO Q.S3.
IF ANY CHILDREN, RECORD ON GRID B AND ASK Q.S2b.

No children in family..........(20(____-1

S2b. How many of them are girls?

RECORD ON GRID B

Grid B
Circle Number of Children in Household

	1	2	3	4	5	6+
0	MALE	YOUNGER MALE	2ND YOUNGEST MALE	2ND YOUNGEST MALE	2ND YOUNGEST MALE	4TH OLDEST MALE
1	FEMALE	MALE	OLDEST MALE	2ND YOUNGEST MALE	2ND YOUNGEST MALE	3RD OLDEST MALE
2	✗	YOUNGER FEMALE	YOUNGEST FEMALE	OLDEST MALE	2ND YOUNGEST MALE	2ND OLDEST MALE
3	✗	✗	2ND YOUNGEST FEMALE	YOUNGEST FEMALE	OLDER MALE	OLDEST MALE
4	✗	✗	✗	2ND YOUNGEST FEMALE	YOUNGEST FEMALE	YOUNGEST FEMALE
5	✗	✗	✗	✗	2ND YOUNGEST FEMALE	2ND YOUNGEST FEMALE
6+	✗	✗	✗	✗	✗	4TH OLDEST FEMALE

S2C. Which adult in the family knows the most about the health care for (CHILD SELECTED BY GRID B)?

RECORD NAME BELOW FOR "CHILD PROXY"

S3. (IF "ADULT DESIGNATED RESPONDENT" OR "CHILD PROXY" IS ALREADY ON THE PHONE, CONDUCT THAT INTERVIEW FIRST. IF NEITHER ON PHONE, ASK: I need to interview (ADULT DESIGNATED RESPONDENT) and (CHILD PROXY)). Is either of them home now?

IF ONE RESPONDENT HOME, CONDUCT APPROPRIATE INTERVIEW AND MAKE APPOINTMENT OR FIND OUT THE BEST TIME TO CALL BACK FOR THE OTHER INTERVIEW

IF NEITHER IS HOME, GET NAMES FOR BOTH RESPONDENTS AND MAKE APPOINTMENTS OR FIND OUT BEST TIME TO CALL BACK.

IF ADULT DESIGNATED RESPONDENT IS IN THE HOSPITAL, A NURSING HOME, OR IS INCAPACITATED BY ILLNESS, OR ADULT SELECTED BY GRID DOES NOT SPEAK ENGLISH OR SPANISH, ASK TO SPEAK TO ADULT WHO IS THE MOST KNOWLEDGEABLE ABOUT THAT PERSON'S HEALTH CARE. RECORD NAME BELOW FOR "PROXY FOR ADULT."

RECORD RESPONDENT NAME(S)   BEST TIME TO CALL BACK:

_____   _____
Adult Designated Respondent

_____   _____
Child Proxy

_____
Proxy for adult in hospital, nursing home, or incapacitated by illness.

EVERYDAY POLLSTERS, INC.
4000 Home St.
Kansas City, Kans. 00001

Study No. 814009

March 1982
Cross Section

01
___ ___
(17-18)

FOR OFFICE USE ONLY:

Questionnaire No.:_____
　　　　　　　　　　5-6-7-8

Sample Point No. _____
10-11-12-13-14-15-16

Interviewer: _____ Date:_____

Telephone No. _____

Hello, I'm _____ from Everyday Pollsters, Inc., the public opinion research company. We're talking to people all over New York City about health care issues facing the public. We're interested in learning more about the medical care that the people of New York need for themselves and their families. I'd like to talk about *your* experiences in getting medical care when you need it. First, I need to ask a few general questions to see if we can include you in our survey. Are you 17 years of age or older? (IF NO, ASK TO SPEAK WITH SOMEONE 17 YEARS OF AGE OR OLDER.)

S1a. Including yourself, how many *adults* 17 years of age or older in your family live in this apartment or living quarters? Please include people who are temporarily in the hospital or who may have entered a nursing home or any other health or convalescent facility in the last six months.

| INTERVIEWER NOTE: IF ANSWER IS "NONE," ASK: May I speak to someone who lives in this household? |

S1b. How many of the adults are females?

| RECORD Q.S1a AND Q.S1b on GRID A |

Grid A

Circle Number of Adults In Household

Circle Number of Adult Females

	1	2	3	4	5	6+
0	MALE	YOUNGER MALE	2ND YOUNGEST MALE	2ND YOUNGEST MALE	2ND YOUNGEST MALE	4TH OLDEST MALE
1	FEMALE	MALE	OLDEST MALE	2ND YOUNGEST MALE	2ND YOUNGEST MALE	3RD OLDEST MALE
2		YOUNGER FEMALE	YOUNGEST FEMALE	OLDEST MALE	2ND YOUNGEST MALE	2ND OLDEST MALE
3			2ND YOUNGEST FEMALE	YOUNGEST FEMALE	OLDER MALE	OLDEST MALE
4				2ND YOUNGEST FEMALE	YOUNGEST FEMALE	YOUNGEST FEMALE
5					2ND YOUNGEST FEMALE	2ND YOUNGEST FEMALE
6+						4TH OLDEST FEMALE

S1c. Could you give me the first name or initials of (DESIGNATED RESPONDENT IN GRID A)?

| RECORD NAME FOR "ADULT DESIGNATED RESPONDENT" AT BOTTOM OF PAGE 1 |

19Z

FOR FIELD USE:	TOTAL COMPLETE .... _____
	ADULT COMPLETE, NEED CHILD PROXY .. _____
	CHILD PROXY COMPLETE, NEED ADULT .. _____
	CALL BACK ADULT................................... _____
	CALL BACK CHILD PROXY .... _____
	CALL BACK BOTH .... _____
	CALL BACK (SPECIFY)............................... _____

- Give them several "problems" to be sure they can follow the instructions. Example: Suppose five adults live in the house and three are females. How would you indicate this? Who is the designated respondent? Example: How would you record six adults in the household; five females at home and one in a nursing home? Who is the designated respondent?

When You Should Collect The Data And Return It To Us

Every manual should include a schedule and calendar. Here's a small portion of a data collector's schedule:

NOVEMBER	Obtain a resume from each teacher, the principal and administrator.
Nov. 28 - Dec. 2	Schedule principal's interview for week of Dec. 12-16. Send out interview form.
	Complete **Review of Resumes**.
DECEMBER	Begin collecting data about in-service training on a weekly basis starting this month.
	Complete **Participant Observations** during this month at your own pace.
Dec. 5 - 9	Return completed **Review of Resumes**.
Dec. 12 - 16	Interview principal. Ask principal to check completed form for accuracy.
	Ask principal to schedule interview with financial officer for week of Jan. 9-13.
Dec. 19 - 23	Send copy of completed **Principal Interview** to evaluator.

Keeping Your Act Together: Monitoring And Support

To make sure you're getting the most accurate data possible, you should monitor all field activities. This might mean something as informal as having the data collectors call you once a week or something as formal as submitting a standardized checklist of activities each day. To nip problems in the bud, you might want to:

- Establish a "Hotline." If you have data collectors who are outside the local area, you may want to provide them with telephone assistance.

- Provide scripts. If the data collectors have to introduce themselves or the study, give them a script or a set of topics to cover.

- Make sure you give out extra copies of all supplementary materials. If data collectors are to mail survey questionnaires back to you, for example, make sure to give them extra questionnaires and envelopes.

- Provide an easy-to-read hand-out describing the program and the evaluation.

This lesson is reprinted from the September 1983 issue of How To Evaluate Education Programs.

NOTES

Lesson 5

How To Choose A Survey Design

What do these four people have in common?

1. A school board candidate wants to find out about the issues that are bothering his area's voters. How do they feel about merit pay? Should there be nongraded classrooms? What new programs should he support?

2. A publisher of high school science textbooks wants to know why some teachers prefer one chemistry book while others prefer another. How do the teachers in the first group compare to those in the second in terms of age, experience and education? How many majored in chemistry in college?

3. Before designing a new lunch program, a nutritionist wants to find out about students' dietary habits so that the school's ethnic diversity is respected. What do students commonly eat for lunch? What do they know about nutrition?

4. The assistant superintendent for vocational education wants to know how students who participated in a special career education program view work in general. Do they believe work is just to earn money? Do they take on-the-job conflicts personally? Did their attitudes change over time?

If you said that the school board candidate, textbook publisher, nutritionist and superintendent share a need to poll or survey the opinions of their constituents, you were correct.

A survey is a method of gathering information from a sample of people to learn something about the larger population from which the sample is drawn.

The school board candidate who wants to find out about the issues bothering his areas's voters will have to learn the rules of survey research. These will enable him to select a valid sample to poll by telling him how many people are "enough" to make accurate evaluations of the voters' concerns.

The rules will help him with questions like: How many men and women should be in my sample, since I know that more women in the area vote than do men? Should I select an equal number of people from each of the area's five districts even if some have larger populations than others?

In this lesson, we are going to discuss several commonly used survey research designs. For technical details like sample size and selection, you can consult a standard text like Survey Research Methods, by Earl R. Babbie (Wadsworth Publishing Company, Belmont, California: 1973).

For the kind of survey most school people will want to do, however, the idea is to get as many responses as you possibly can. The closer you come to getting everybody in the survey group to respond, the more likely you are to have answers everyone will accept.

Cross-sectional Surveys

With this design, data are collected at a single point in time to describe a population. Think of a cross-sectional survey as a snapshot of a group of people or organizations. Suppose the school board candidate wants to know if he'll win. Consider this question and its answer:

Question: If the school board elections were held today, for whom would you vote?
Sample: A cross section of eligible voters in the Hart Central School District.
Method: Telephone interviews conducted by trained volunteers.
Answer: If the elections were held today, Candidate X would undoubtedly win. Here's proof (using hypothetical data):

Table 1: Preferences for a School Board Candidate by Men and Women Voters

	Men		Women		Total of Men and Women	
	Number	Percent	Number	Percent	Number	Percent
Candidate X	168	34	175	35	357	69
Candidate Y	75	15	50	10	97	25
Candidate Z	21	4	11	2	46	6
Totals	**264**	**53**	**236**	**47**	**500**	**100**

Table 2: Preferences for a School Board Candidate by Voters' Occupation

	Teachers and School Administrators		Business, Medical, Legal		Others		Total	
	Number	Percent	Number	Percent	Number	Percent	Number	Percent
Candidate X	99	20	96	19	41	8	236	47
Candidate Y	35	7	37	7	90	18	162	32
Candidate Z	47	9	52	10	3	1	102	21
Totals	**181**	**36**	**185**	**37**	**134**	**27**	**500**	**100**

Assuming that a sample of voters has been wisely chosen and the right questions have been asked, Tables 1 and 2 reveal that Candidate X is a winner.

Here's why:

1. Regardless of sex or occupation, Candidate X is ahead.
2. More men than women prefer candidates Y and Z. But when it comes to X, men and women have nearly the same preferences.
3. "Other" voters preferred Candidate Y, but there are not so many of them as voters in the other two categories who preferred Candidate X.

Of course, you might want to use only Table 1 or just Table 2 to make your point. But it is often useful to analyze and present survey data in categories that you think are important.

With the voter-preference data, for example, you might also have considered age (Do the younger voters have a preference?), political party (How do registered Democrats compare with registered Republicans?), or place of residence (How do people in this part of town compare with people in other other part?).

Cross-sectional surveys have several advantages. First, they describe things as they are and provide a good basis for planning. If you're unhappy with the picture a cross-sectional survey reveals, you can change it. Cross-sectional surveys are also relatively easy to do, once you've mastered the rules of survey research. They are limited, however, in that if things change rapidly, you could find yourself acting on outdated information.

Longitudinal Surveys

With longitudinal survey designs, you collect data over time. At least three designs are particularly useful.

Trend Designs

A trend design means surveying a particular group (say sixth graders) over time--once a year for three years. Of course, the first group of sixth graders will become seventh graders next year, so you're really sampling different groups of children. You are assuming that the information you need about sixth graders will remain consistent over the three-year period.

Look at this:

<u>Question</u>: What do sixth graders know about health?
<u>Sample</u>: Sixth graders in Hart Central School District.
<u>Method</u>: Self-administered questionnaires distributed and supervised by teachers.
<u>Answer</u>: Sixth graders consistently know little about disease prevention, they're beginning to learn about nutrition and they appear to know the causes of disease.

Proof (using some more hypothetical data) is displayed in Table 3.

As with cross-sectional studies, you could have analyzed the results of the health survey by comparing boys and girls, different schools, teachers, and so on.

Table 3: Sixth Graders' Knowledge of Three Health Topics
(N = 1,652)

	Causes of Disease	Nutrition	Prevention
1982	Little	Little	Little
1983	Some	Some	Little
1984	Much	Some	Little

Source: Scores on the "Health Information Scale" (HIS), Level 6: Health Survey Foundation, Los Angeles, California: 1981.

Note: This is a fictitious table for illustration only. Sample items from the hypothetical HIS appear on page 46.

Cohort Designs

In cohort designs, you study a particular group over time, but the people in the group may vary. Suppose, for example, you wanted to study certain students' attitudes toward work because they had participated in a special career education program.

You might survey a random sample of the program's graduates in 1984, and then in 1994, choose a second random sample from the 1984 graduates and survey them. Although the second sample might turn out to be entirely different from the first, you'd still be describing the attitudes of the class of 1984.

Think about this example, where evaluators followed students from the class of 1965 to find out about their attitudes toward work and how those attitudes changed over time:

Question: How have students' attitudes toward work changed since 1965?
Sample: 1965 high school seniors from Hart Central School District.
Method: Mailed self-administered questionnaires.
Answer: In general, attitudes toward work have improved dramatically since 1965. No relationship was found between sex and attitude, however. In 1965 and 1975, girls had poorer attitudes than boys, but the situation was reversed in 1970 and 1980. For proof, see Figure 1.

As can be seen from the figure, boys' and girls' attitudes fluctuated with time, although they both got better. What happened? Unless the researchers systematically monitor the events that affect the class of 1965, they won't be able to tell from the survey results.

The only way to comprehend fully the cause of events is to put together large-scale experimental studies that conform to scientific methods for gathering reliable and valid evidence.

Are the differences between boys and girls meaningful? This question is a little easier to answer, since information from technically sound surveys is amenable to statistical analysis. You might compare boys and girls over time with respect to their views on work by using analysis of variance techniques.

Figure 1: Class of 1965's Attitude Toward Work

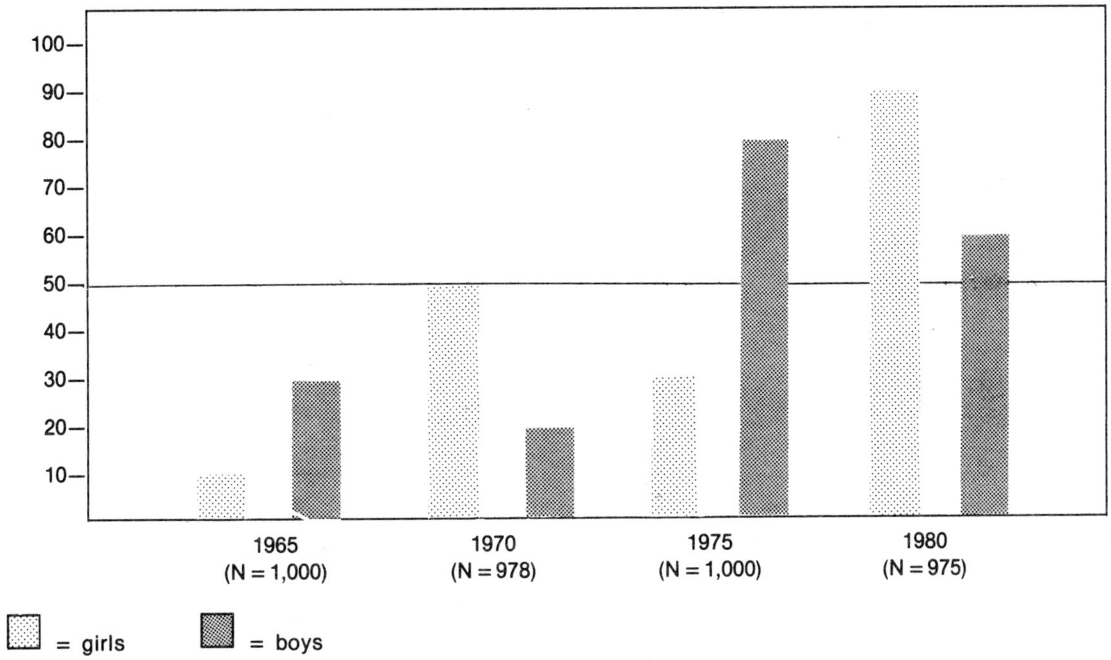

```
100—
 90—
 80—
 70—
 60—
 50—
 40—
 30—
 20—
 10—
      1965        1970        1975        1980
    (N=1,000)   (N=978)    (N=1,000)    (N=975)
```

☐ = girls   ▓ = boys

Source: "Attitude Toward Work Inventory," McConnell Publishing, New York, N.Y.: 1960.
Note: This is a fictitious table for illustration only.

Using the scores from Figure 1, the resulting table might look like this:

Table 4: Comparison of Boys' and Girls' Attitudes Toward Work

	Number Of Boys	Number Of Girls	Is the difference in attitude statistically significant*
1980	490	485	Yes
1975	500	500	Yes
1970	490	488	No
1965	500	500	No

* Using ANOVA, p<.01
Source: "Attitude Toward Work Inventory," McConnell Publishing, New York, N.Y.: 1960.
Note: This is a fictitious table for illustration.

Table 4 suggests that with time, the attitudes of boys and girls are significantly different from one another, although both improve. Why this should be or why the girls and boys change places cannot be determined from the hypothetical data in the table.

Panel Designs

Panel designs mean collecting data from the same sample over time. If you were concerned with monitoring the attitudes toward work of the high school class of 1965, you would select a sample of students and follow them and only them throughout the desired time period.

One way to display the results of your data is shown in Figure 2.

The figure suggests a real improvement in attitude. To find out whether the improvement is significant, however, you must test it statistically, just as in the example for cohort studies. Another observation from this figure is that the improvement might be leveling off. Again, you cannot tell why, and without further surveys, you won't know whether students' attitudes have reached their ceiling.

Longitudinal surveys show growth in ideas and attitudes. They aren't used frequently, but when they are successful, they're very convincing.

Longitudinal surveys do have their disadvantages, however. They're expensive because they require repeated administrations of a survey instrument. Their rigor is subject to wear and tear as time passes. How accurate can a longitudinal survey be if people move out of your reach or refuse to participate? Finally, they can be complicated. Keeping track of a panel, for example, is time consuming and logistically confusing.

Sample Items

We've referred to two hypothetical survey instruments in this lesson. To give you an idea of what they might look like, here are some hypothetical sample items.

From the hypothetical Health Information Scale:

1. Which of the following can cause pneumonia?
    A. Bacteria
    B. Too much exercise
    C. Smoking
    D. Poor eating habits

2. Which of the following is a drug?
    A. Alcohol
    B. Soda pop
    C. Milk
    D. Chocolate
3. How many different food groups are there?
    A. 3
    B. 4
    C. 5
    D. 6

From the hypothetical Attitude Toward Work Inventory:

Figure 2: Class of 1965's Attitude Toward Work
(N = 1,000)

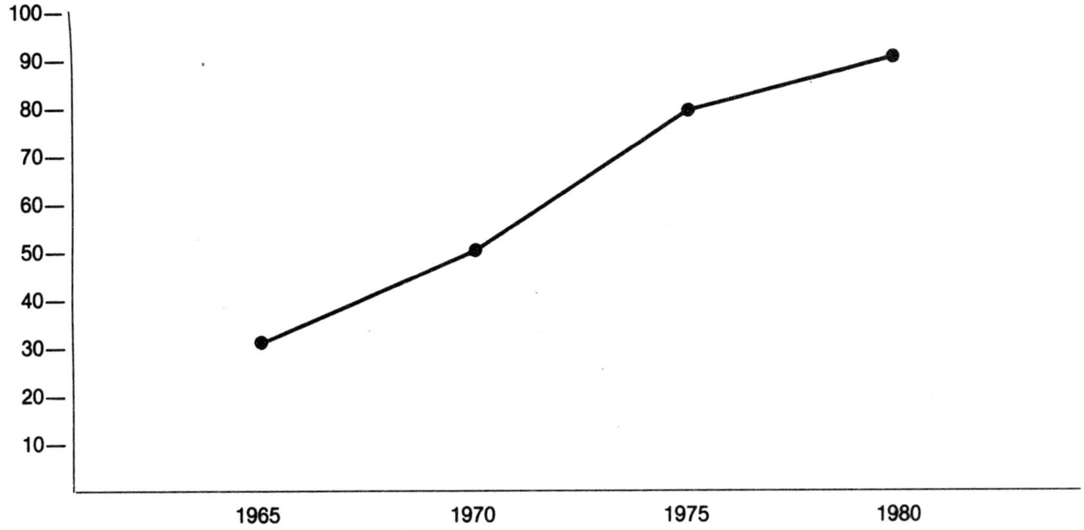

Source: "Attitude Toward Work Inventory," McConnell Publishing, New York, N.Y.: 1960.
Note: This is a fictitious table for illustration only.

This lesson is reprinted from the June 1984 issue of *How To Evaluate Education Programs.*

NOTES

Lesson 6

How To Conduct A Survey

Surveys are a popular way to collect evaluation information because they are relatively inexpensive and provide quick results. More important, they tend to be easy to participate in and understand. Don't forget, however, that surveys also have their technical side. If you ignore the rules of survey research, you will probably get unreliable information. The American Statistical Association (ASA) publication, "What is a Survey?" sets out the guideposts for conducting reliable surveys and understanding their uses.

What Is A Survey?

A survey is a way to gather information from a sample group of people to learn something about the larger population from which the sample has been drawn. Thus, you might survey a community to find out about its interests in higher education or poll students in a school to see what they think about a new approach to science education.

Surveys come in many different forms and have many different aims, but they do share certain characteristics. Unlike a census of an entire population, they collect information from only a small group of people (or schools, districts or other units, depending on the purpose of the study). "In a bona fide survey, the sample is not selected haphazardly or only from persons who volunteer to participate. It is scientifically chosen so that each individual in the population has a known chance of selection. In this way, the results can be reliably projected to the larger public," says the ASA.

Surveys use standardized questions so that everyone surveyed responds to exactly the same question. The purpose of a survey is not to describe the particular people who happen to be part of the sample, but to get a statistical profile of the population. "Individual respondents," says the ASA, "are never identified and the survey's results are presented in the form of summaries, such as statistical tables and charts."

The sample size required for a survey depends on the reliability needed. The reliability you need, in turn, depends on how you will use the results. There is no simple rule that you can follow for all surveys, but experts say a moderate sample size is usually sufficient. "For example, the well-known national polls generally use samples of about 1,500 persons to reflect national attitudes and opinions. A sample of this size produces accurate estimates even for a country as large as the United States with a population of over 200 million."

When you stop to think that a properly selected sample of only 1,500 people can reflect different characteristics of the total population within a very small margin of error, it is easy to understand the value of surveys.

Different Kinds Of Surveys

"Surveys can be classified in a number of ways," says the ASA. One way is by size and type of sample. Many surveys study the total adult population, but yours might focus on special population groups, such as teachers, students or principals. Surveys may be conducted nationally, statewide, or locally, seeking the responses of a few hundred or many thousands of people.

Another way to classify surveys is by the way they collect data, such as by mail, telephone and personal interview. Newer methods of data collection record information directly into computers. One example of this is when TV audiences are measured by devices that automatically record in a computer the channels watched on a sample group of TV sets.

"Mail surveys are seldom used to collect information from the general public because names and addresses are not often available and the response rate tends to be low," the ASA says. Yet this method may be highly effective with members of particular groups, such as members of a professional association.

Telephone interviewing is becoming more popular, as it is an efficient method of collecting some types of data. Although a personal interview in a respondent's home or office is much more costly than a telephone survey, you may have to resort to this when you need to collect complex information.

Surveys also can be classified by their content. Some surveys, such as pre-election voter surveys, focus on opinions and attitudes, while others try to identify characteristics or behavior, such as level of education or reading habits.

Many surveys include both kinds of questions. Thus, you might ask a respondent "if s(he) has heard or read about an issue, what s(he) knows about it, her (his) opinion, how strongly s(he) feels and why," says ASA. But you might also need certain factual information to help you classify the responses, such as age, sex, marital status, occupation and place of residence.

"The questions may be open ended ('Why do you feel that way?') or closed ('Do you approve or disapprove?'); they may ask the respondent to rate a political candidate or a product on some kind of scale; they may ask for a ranking of various alternatives. The questionnaire may be very brief--a few questions taking five minutes or less, or it can be quite long--requiring an hour or more" to complete.

Designing A Survey

The first step in planning a survey is to decide what your objectives are. These should be specific, clear cut and as unambiguous as possible. Next, you will have to develop the methodology for carrying out the survey. How will you define and locate eligible respondents? What method will you use to collect the data? You will have to design and pretest a questionnaire, develop procedures to minimize response errors, design and select appropriate samples, and hire and train interviewers (unless you are using self-administered questionnaires). You will have to decide how to handle cases in which you get no response and make plans for tabulating and analyzing responses.

Designing the questionnaire is one of the most critical stages in survey development, according to the ASA. "The questionnaire links the information need to the realized measurement.

Survey Sampling Considerations

Virtually all surveys for policymakers employ some form of scientific sampling. Even the decennial Censuses of Population and Housing use sampling techniques for gathering most of the data, although 100 percent enumeration is used for the basic population counts. "Methods of sampling are well-grounded in statistical theory and in the theory of probability," the ASA says, so you can feel just as confident with a carefully constructed sample as you would with the entire population, provided a large proportion of the sample answers the survey.

The particular type of sample to use depends on your survey objectives, the overall survey budget, how you will collect data, the subject matter and the kind of respondent you need. The first thing to do is to define the target population. This can be all the people in the entire nation or all the people in a certain city, or it can be a subset such as all teenagers in a given location. The target population need not be people; it may be libraries, schools or government agencies, and so on.

The types of samples range from simple random selection of units to highly complex samples with multiple levels of selection stratification and clustering into various groups. Whether simple or complex, a properly designed sample means that "all the units in the target population have a known, nonzero chance of being included," says the ASA. What's more, the sample design must be described in sufficient detail to permit reasonably accurate calculation of sampling errors. These are the features that make it scientifically valid to draw inferences from the sample results about the entire population that the sample represents.

Ideally, you would choose the sample size according to how reliable the final estimates must be. In practice, you usually have to make a trade-off between the ideal sample size and the expected cost of the survey.

Crucial to sample design and selection is defining the source from which to draw a sample. This source, termed the sampling frame, generally is a list of some kind, such as a list of schools in a city or a list of students in a university. If there is no list, the sampling frame also can consist of geographic areas with well-defined natural or artificial boundaries. In this case you select a sample of geographic areas called segments and canvass them to make a list for the appropriate units--households, retail stores or whatever--so that you can include some or all of them in the final sample.

The sampling frame also can consist of less concrete things, such as all possible permutations of integers that make up banks of telephone numbers, if you want to include unlisted numbers in telephone surveys. The quality of the sampling frame--whether it is up to date and complete--is probably the most important factor in making sure you have adequate coverage of the desired population.

Administering The Survey

No matter how well you design your survey, it will be wasted if it's not properly executed. Interviewers must be carefully trained on such points as how to make initial contacts, how to conduct interviews in a professional manner and how to avoid influencing or biasing responses. The training generally involves practice in the kind of situations interviewers are likely to encounter. Each interviewer should have survey materials, including ample copies of the questionnaire, a reference manual, information about how to identify and locate respondents, and any cards or pictures to be used.

Before the interview, you may want to send a letter to the sample members explaining the survey's purpose and that an interviewer will be calling soon. In many surveys, especially those sponsored by the federal government, you must tell the respondent the survey is voluntary or mandatory and how the answers are to be used.

Try to schedule calls or visits at the best time of day to catch respondents, eliminating as many call-backs as possible. Control the quality of the field work by rechecking a sample of interviews and by setting up office procedures to detect missing data or obvious mistakes.

Before you can compute aggregated totals, averages or other statistics from completed questionnaires, they must be coded and keypunched, entered directly onto tape to create a computer file, or entered directly into the computer. By then you will need to decide how to treat missing data and "not answered" items.

Errors in coding, keypunching and transcription must be rigorously controlled through checking. Once a computer file has been generated, it's possible to do additional computer editing to alter inconsistent or impossible entries, such as a six-year-old grandfather.

After you have a "clean file," you can tell a computer programmer what kind of analysis you need--frequency counts, cross-tabulations or more sophisticated methods of data analysis--to help answer the objectives of the survey.

The results are usually published or explained at staff briefings or more formal meetings. Secondary analyses also are possible if you make computer data files available to others at nominal costs.

Survey Pitfalls

Avoid shortcuts. It may be simple and cheap to select a sample of names from the phone book, but you lose all the people who have unlisted numbers or no phone. Be sure to use a pretest even though it takes additional time, because you can't foresee the misunderstandings that even the simplest questions create. Failure to follow up nonrespondents (by phone, mail, or visit) also can ruin a survey. A low response rate in a big sample does more damage than having a small sample in the first place since there is no valid way to infer the characteristics of the population represented by nonrespondents. Finally, make sure that you have good quality control at all stages. Check to see that interviewers, for example, are asking the same questions in the same way. Retrain them when necessary.

Here are some sources of survey bias to avoid:

- Sampling operations. Errors in sample selection or through omitting part of the population from the sample form.

- Lack of knowledge. Respondents sometimes do not know or remember the information requested.

- Concealment of the truth. Fear or suspicion may cause respondents to conceal the truth.

- Loaded questions. The question may be worded to influence the respondents to answer in a specific (not necessarily correct) way.

- Processing errors. These can include coding errors, data keying, computer programming errors, etc.

- Conceptual problems. For example, the population or the time period may not be the one you need, but had to be used to meet a deadline.

- Interviewer errors. Interviewers may misread the question or twist the answers.

One way to get respondents to cooperate is to ensure that their answers will be kept confidential. To safeguard confidentiality you should:

- Use only code numbers for the identity of a respondent on a questionnaire and keep the code separate from the questionnaires.

- Refuse to give out names and addresses of survey respondents.

- Destroy questionnaires and identifying information about respondents after the responses have been put onto computer tape.

- Omit the names and addresses of survey respondents from computer tapes used for analysis.

- Present statistical tabulations by broad enough categories that individual respondents cannot be singled out.

Survey Costs

The costs of a survey, the ASA says, should cover:

1. Staff time for planning the study and steering it through the various stages.

2. Labor and material for pretesting the questionnaire and field procedures.

3. Hiring, training and supervising interviewers.

4. Interviewer labor and travel expenses (and meals and lodging, if out of town).

5. Labor and expenses for checking a certain percentage of the interviews (by doing them over).

6. Preparing codes for transferring information from the questionnaires.

7. Labor and materials for editing, coding and keypunching the information from the questionnaires onto computer tape.

8. Do spot checks to make sure of the quality of the editing, coding and keypunching.

9. "Cleaning" the final data tapes, (i.e., checking the tapes for inconsistent or impossible answers).

10. Programming tabulations and special analyses of the data.

11. Computer time for the various tabulations and analyses.

12. Labor time and materials for analyzing the data and preparing the report.

13. Telephone charges, postage, reproduction and printing.

Try This

<u>What is wrong with the following survey plan?</u> The Newcastle School District is conducting a survey of parents with children in its high schools to find out if the total curriculum is considered adequate, and if not, why. The results of the survey will be used to help decide on graduation requirements. To save the cost of field testing, the survey form will be similar to one already used in the Foundation Hill School District. The form will go to a random sample of parents. The sampling plan involves selecting every 12th parent on the district's roster. To cut the time required to complete the survey, some of the forms include a few important questions, while the rest contain a longer list. The response rate is expected to be high in this "education conscious" community, so no follow-up is planned.

Answer 1. Although the survey form worked well for the Fountain Hill School District, Newcastle District officials cannot be sure it will work for them. There may be real, although not obvious, differences between the two districts.

2. Choosing every 12th (or any other number) name from a list of names is not random assignment. "Random" selection means that everyone has an equal chance of being chosen.

3. With few exceptions, all survey forms should ask the same questions in the same way.

References

Ferber, Robert, et. al. "What Is A Survey?" Washington, D.C.: American Statistical Association, 1980.

This lesson is reprinted from the August 1985 issue of
How To Evaluate Education Programs.

NOTES

Lesson 7

How To Use The Normal Curve

How familiar to you are words like standard deviation, percentile, standardo score and normal distribution? If you are a student, a teacher, or an evaluator, you probably answered "very," even though these are highly technical terms.

Here are some examples of how you might hear them used:

Student: "My score was 650, which means I'm one standard deviation above the mean on the verbal test."

Teacher: "Our science class performs at the 55th percentile, just above the average in our state."

Evaluator: "My data are not normally distributed and don't resemble a bell-shaped curve, so I will rely on a nonparametric statistic."

We are devoting this chapter to the normal distribution, or the famous bell-shaped curve. It is the basis for deriving percentiles, standard scores and stanines, and is a requirement for using statistical techniques such as analysis of variance (ANOVA).

Table 1—Frequency Table of Math Scores (N = 115)

Interval of Scores	Midpoint	Frequency
1-10	5.5	3
11-20	15.5	6
21-30	25.5	16
31-40	35.5	20
41-50	45.5	25
51-60	55.5	25
61-70	65.5	14
71-80	75.5	4
81-90	85.5	2
95-100	95.5	1

Starting With Frequency Distributions

Suppose Table 1 (previous page) shows the frequency counts for scores on a math test given to 115 tenth-grade students. The first column gives the range of possible scores on the test, divided into intervals of ten points. The next column gives the midpoints--for example, the middle point between a score of 1 and 10 is 5.5. The third column gives the frequency--for instance, three students had scores between 1 and 10 points.

To see how the scores on the math test are distributed among students, it's helpful to construct a histogram or frequency plot. A histogram looks like a bar graph, showing the number of scores for each interval (see Figure 1).

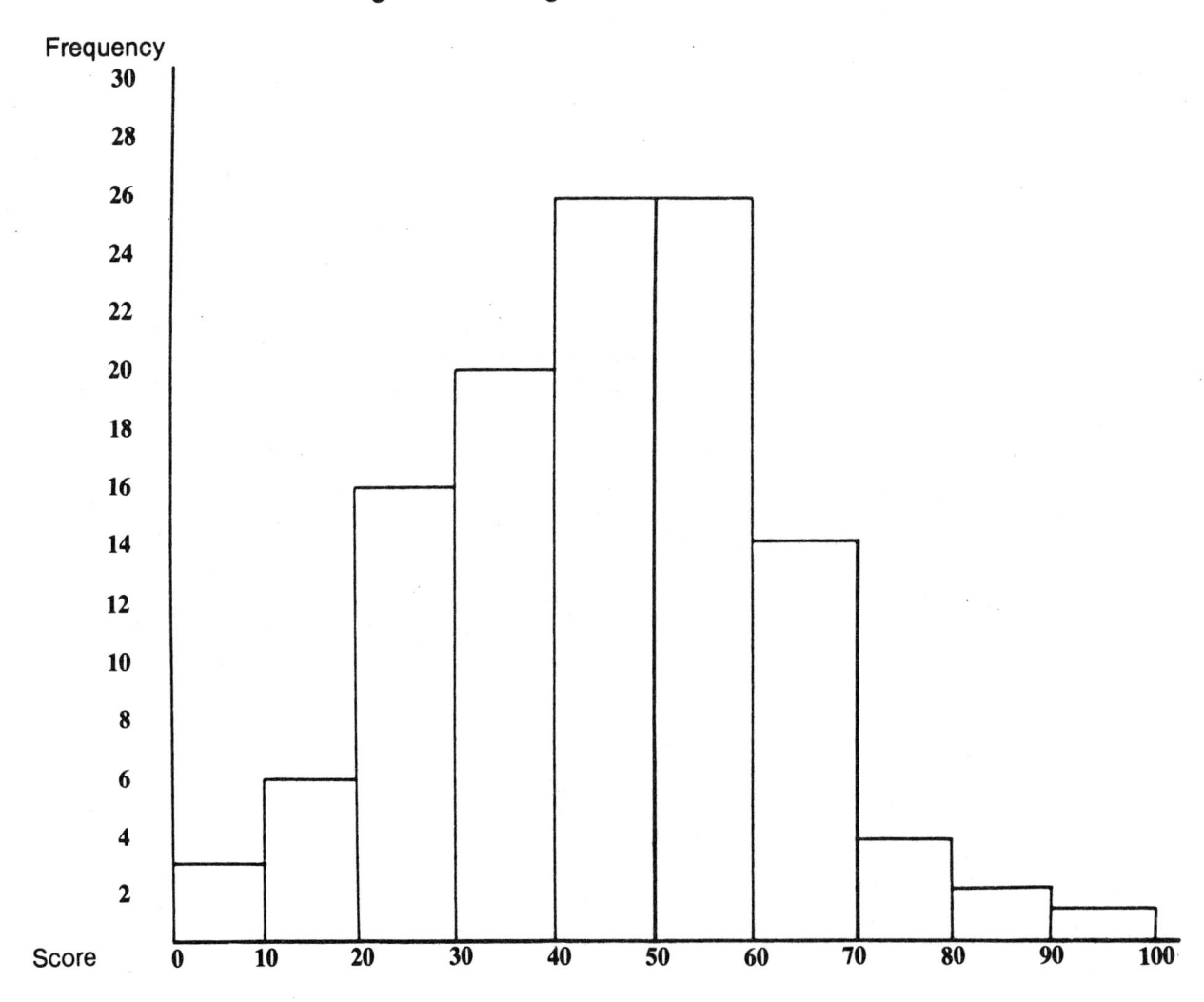

Figure 1—Histogram of Scores on Math Test

A frequency plot is similar to a histogram, but with a line connecting the midpoints of adjacent intervals, as in Figure 2.

Now suppose you gave the same math test to thousands of students and summarized the data just as in Table 1, except that you used smaller and smaller intervals. This would produce more refined information, and the

How To Use The Normal Curve

frequency plots would begin to resemble a continuous curve. Such a surve is called a frequency curve or frequency distribution.

Mathematically, it helps to approximate or describe the distribution of scores by using frequency curves. One advantage of frequency distributions is that you can obtain various areas or proportions under the curves from mathematical tables. Another is that if scores fall into some well-known frequency curve, many characteristics of the distribution are known immediately.

Figure 2—Frequency Plot of Math Scores

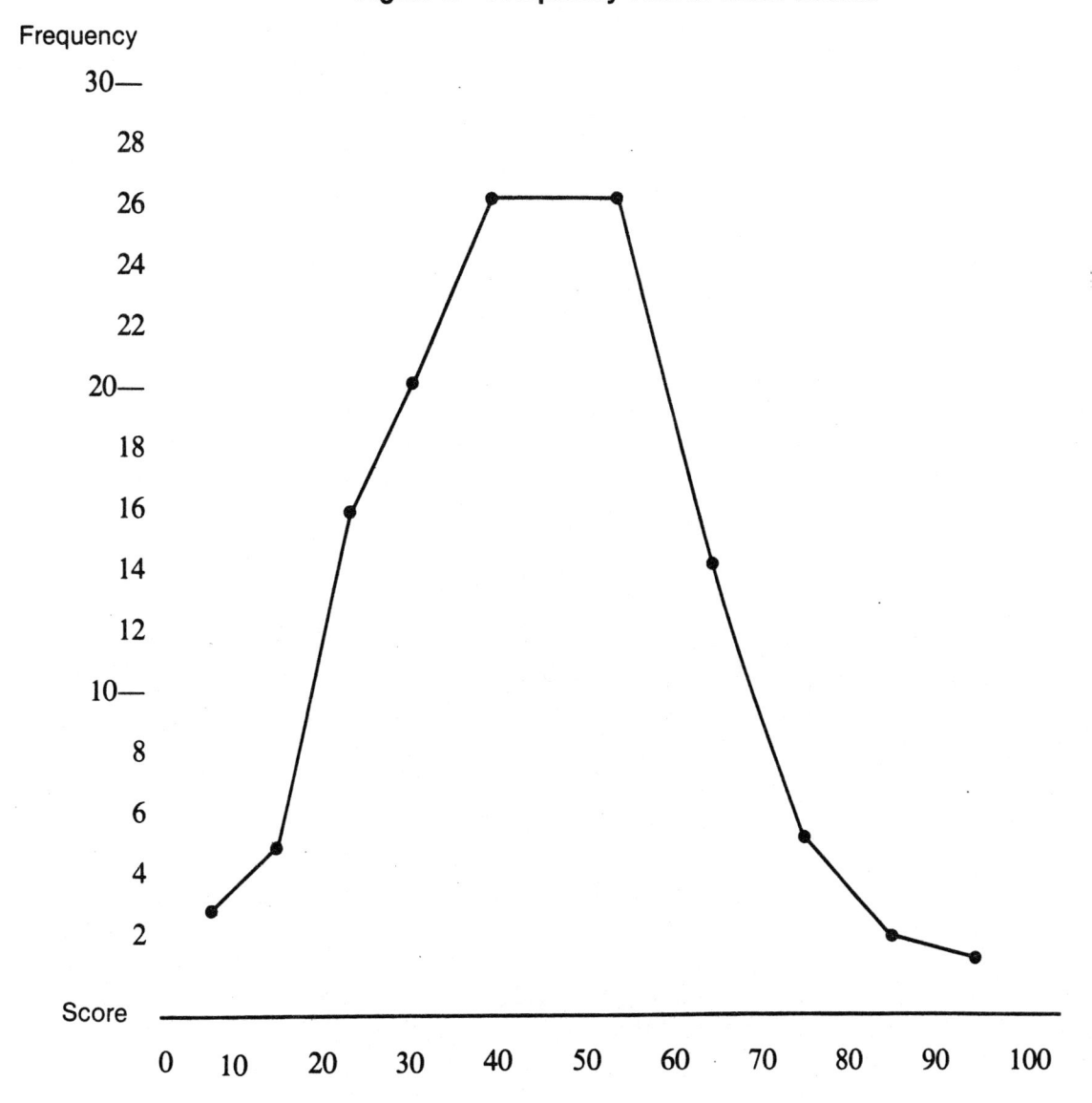

In statistics, the most famous and commonly used of all frequency curves is the normal distribution (see Figure 3, next page).

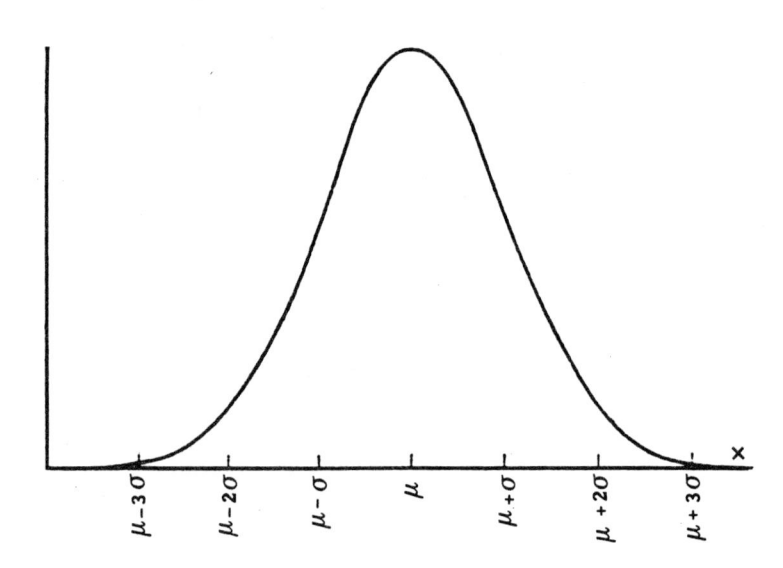

Figure 3—Typical Normal Distribution

[Bell curve with x-axis labeled: $\mu-3\sigma$, $\mu-2\sigma$, $\mu-\sigma$, μ, $\mu+\sigma$, $\mu+2\sigma$, $\mu+3\sigma$]

Characteristics Of The Normal Curve

Although the normal distribution is defined by the equation of its curve, you don't have to know the mathematics to understand the distribution. Just think of the curve itself as defining the distribution.

To say that a variable like math test scores is normally distributed means that an infinite population of math scores has a frequency curve that is symmetrical and bell-shaped, as seen in Figure 3. The curve extends an infinite distance in both directions but comes very close to the horizontal axis.

The normal curve has two parameters that describe it completely, the mean and the variance (or its square root, the standard deviation). The Greek letters μ (mu) and σ (sigma) are used to represent the mean and standard deviation of theoretical frequency distributions. (When computing frequency distributions for samples or subsets of the total population, the mean and standard deviation are usually represented as $\bar{x}$ and S.D.)

What Is The Standard Deviation?

Everyone who reads about tests has heard the term "standard deviation." What does it mean? It's the square root of the variance of the scores.

Here's how Prof. Arthur R. Jensen explains it in his book, <u>Plain Talk About Mental Tests</u> (Copyright 1981 by the Free Press, a Division of Macmillan Publishing Co., Inc.):

"To calculate the variance of a set of scores, you first determine the arithmetic mean, which is the sum of all the scores divided by the total number of scores. From each score you next substract the mean and square the remainder. Then you sum all these squares and, finally, divide by the total number of scores. These operations are expressed more simply in mathematical notation as

$$S^2 = \sum (x - \bar{x})^2/N$$

where S^2 is the variance, $\sum$ means "the sum of," x is a test score, $\bar{x}$ is the mean of all the scores, and N is the total number of scores.

If a variance is normally distributed, then:

(1) The area under the normal curve between $\mu - \sigma$ and $\mu + \sigma$ (e.g., one standard deviation unit on either side of the mean) is 68% of the total area.

(2) The area under the normal curve between $\mu - 2\sigma$ and $\mu + 2\sigma$ (e.g., two standard deviation units on either side of the mean) is 95% of the total area.

(3) The area under the normal curve between $\mu - 3\sigma$ and $\mu + 3\sigma$ (e.g., three standard deviation units on either side of the mean) is 99.7% of the total area.

Notice that the horizontal axis in Figure 3 has been marked off in units of σ, starting with the mean μ. There is almost no area under the curve beyond 3σ units from μ. But the equation of the curve actually extends in both directions toward infinity, coming extremely close to the horizontal axis.

Figure 4 shows the percentage of area falling into each half of the normal curve.

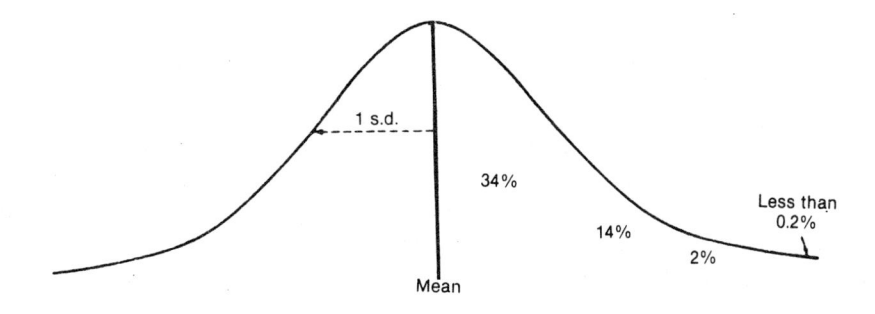

A special property of the normal curve is that its location and shape are completely determined by its values of μ and σ. The value of μ centers the curve, and the value of σ determines the extent of the spread. Since all normal curves representing theoretical frequency distributions have the same total area, as σ increases, the curve must decrease in height and spread out.

This is illustrated in Figures 5 and 6, which are sketches of two normal curves with the same mean, namely 0, and different standard deviations, 1 and 3 respectively. As an evaluator comparing these two curves, you should notice that although the mean μ is the same in both curves, the average score in Figure 5 is much closer to the mean. In other words, there is more homogeneity (and less variance) in the scores represented in Figure 5 than those in Figure 6.

Figure 5—A Standard Normal Distribution with $\mu = 0$ and $\sigma = 1$

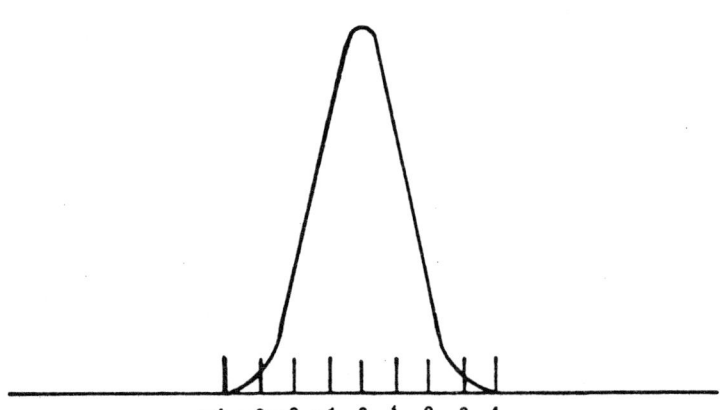

Figure 6—A Normal Distribution with $\mu = 0$ and $\sigma = 3$

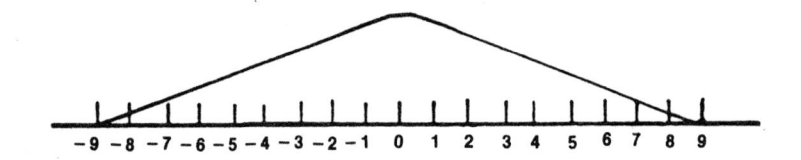

The Standard Normal Curve

Since the shape of a normal curve is determined by μ and σ, you can reduce all normal curves to a standard one simply by changing a variable. For example, the curve in Figure 5 can be made to look like the curve in Figure 6 by changing the scale on the horizontal axis so that one unit on the Figure 5 horizontal axis represents 3 units on the Figure 6 axis. Similarly, Figure 6 could be made like Figure 5 by compressing the Figure 6 axis to one-third its natural length.

The simplest normal curve is one with $\mu = 0$ and $\sigma = 1$. This is called the standard normal curve. In statistics texts, it is the reference curve and all normal curves are usually transformed into this one.

For any point on the horizontal axis of a given normal curve, there is a corresponding point on the standard normal curve. For example, the point x = 6 in Figure 6 corresponds to the point x = 2 in Figure 5, the standard normal curve. Therefore, the value x = 6 in Figure 5 is two standard deviations to the right of its means.

How To Use The Normal Curve

In general, if a point x on the horizontal axis of a normal curve with mean μ and standard deviation σ corresponds to a point z on the standard normal curve, then the point x is z standard deviation units to the right of μ. This relationship can be expressed mathematically as:

$$x = \mu + z\sigma \quad \text{or} \quad z = \frac{x-\mu}{\sigma}$$

These formulas enable one to find the point z on the standard normal curve that corresponds to any point x on a nonstandard normal curve. Thus the point x = 9 in Figure 6 corresponds to the point z = (9-0)/3=3 in Figure 5. This technique allows all normal curves to be reduced to a single standard one.

This trick is frequently used by evaluators and teachers to compare scores on tests with differing means and standard deviations. Suppose, for example, Table 2 shows Jane's scores on mathematics and reading achievement tests. In which area did she do best?

If we can assume that both tests were normally distributed, and we know the mean and standard deviation of each, then we can transform the scores into z-scores and compare them.

Table 2—Jane's Scores

	Math Test	Reading Test
Jane's Score	71	69
μ	50	45
σ	10	8

$$z \text{ math} = \frac{71 - 50}{10} = 2.1 \qquad z \text{ reading} = \frac{69 - 45}{8} = 3.0$$

As you can see, Jane scored well above average in both cases. But she performed almost one standard deviation better in reading than in math, a fact that a simple comparison of her scores of 71 and 69 could not reveal.

Normal Curve Tables

Statistical tables are available that give the area under any part of the normal curve for the variable z, that is, for the standard normal distribution with μ = 0 and σ = 1. See, for example, <u>Introduction to Mathematical Statistics</u>, Paul G. Hoel, John Wiley & Sons, Inc., 1966.

As an illustration, suppose you wanted to find the area under the standard normal curve from z = 0.0 to z = 1.0. A table like the one in Hoel's text would show that the area to the left of z = 0.0 is .5000 or 50% of the area under the curve. In the same table, the area to the left of z = 1.0 is .8413. Thus, the area between z = 0 and z = 1 is .8413 − .5000 = .3413, so about 34% of the total area is between the mean and one standard deviation above it.

Converting Z-Scores To Percentiles

Whenever you have (or think you have) a normal distribution, it is possible to convert z-scores into percentiles--or vice versa--using the same statistical table.

For example, Jane's z-score on the math test was 2.1, slightly more than one standard deviation above the mean. In the table, it has a value of .9821. That means about 98% of the area under the curve is to the left of this number, so her score is at the 98th percentile.

For reading, Jane's z-score of 3.0 translates into .9987 in the table. Nearly 100% of the area under the curve is to the left, making Jane's score virtually at the 100th percentile.

This lesson is reprinted from the April 1985 issue of
How To Evaluate Education Programs.

NOTES

Lesson 8

How To Weigh Statistical Significance

Sometimes the raw data you collect for an evaluation reveal what seems to be a significant difference between otherwise similar groups. If the difference favors students using some promising new educational approach, for example, it's interesting to find out just how important it really is. Could such results have happened by chance?

Anything that is unlikely to happen by chance is a "statistically significant" event. You can use statistical methods to answer questions like these:

- ▶ If we test 300 light bulbs and find 27 defective, is that rate statistically significant? Do we have problems with the quality of our product?

- ▶ If students in the new math program scored 11.2 points higher on the math achievement test than students in the traditional program, is the difference statistically significant?

To determine statistical significance, you must rely on sampling theory. For example, what is the probability that two random samples of students from the same population would produce mean scores that differ by as much as 11.2 points?

Suppose you decide that a chance happening of one time in 100 is an acceptable risk. This predefined probability ($p<.01$) is called the "level of significance." If the differences you observed would occur no more than one out of 100 times, you can reject the null hypothesis of no difference between groups.

Social scientists usually use the .05 or .01 significance level, meaning that the observed difference in the new math and traditional programs would be considered statistically significant if the difference of 11.2 points would occur by chance (assuming the two groups are random samples from the same population) only 5 times in 100 or 1 time in 100.

This is a good place to suggest using common sense in analyzing statistical differences. Statistically significant results are not always educationally significant, and statistically insignificant results are not always educationally insignificant.

If students in an experimental program did better than those in a control group, how much better? Are the results really striking when you view them as evidence of educational improvement? Is the difference worth the added cost of the new program?

Understanding Type I And Type II Errors

In testing statistical hypotheses, you must establish rules that determine when you will accept or reject a null hypothesis.

Take, for example, a statistical test of an experimental (A) and control (B) reading program, where the null hypothesis is that the mean reading scores for both groups are equal,

$$H_o: \bar{X}_A = \bar{X}_B$$

and the alternative hypothesis is that the mean score for the experimental group is higher,

$$H_1: \bar{X}_A > \bar{X}_B$$

When you apply a statistical test (like the t test) to the data, you don't expect to find "zero differences" in mean scores between the two groups. Instead, the real question is whether the differences are so small that they could have occurred simply by chance. When you select two random samples from the same population, you can expect their mean scores to be close, but not exactly the same.

It's up to you to decide how far apart the scores must be before you're satisfied that the difference is not just an accident. You could choose .10, .05, or .01 as the level of significance, depending on the amount of error you're willing to tolerate in rejecting the null hypothesis.

If you select the .05 level of significance, then about 5 times in 100 you will reject the null hypothesis when it is, in fact, correct. This happens because you are comparing two random samples from the same population, and the probability that they will differ by chance alone is 5% ($p<.05$). This situation is known as a Type I error. It is the probability of rejecting the null hypothesis when it is true.

If the level of significance is .01, then the probability of a Type I error is only 1 in 100, or 1%. You can select a level of significance that would virtually eliminate the chance of a Type I error, but there are serious consequences. The less likely you are to make a Type I error, the more likely you are to make a Type II error.

A Type II error is when you accept a null hypothesis that is, in fact, incorrect. In that case, the difference between the two groups' mean scores doesn't fall within the rejection region (say $p<.05$). But in reality, the groups are not alike and the experimental treatment is better (the alternative hypothesis is true).

The power of a statistical test is the probability of correctly rejecting the null hypothesis. Mathematically, power is equal to Type I minus Type II error. From that formula, you can see that Type I errors, Type II errors and power are interrelated. As the probability of making a Type I error goes down, the probability making a Type II error goes up, but the power of the statistical test goes down.

This means you have to weigh the consequences and decide in advance which risk to take. Is it better to risk declaring the experimental group the victor when there is actually no difference between them (a Type I error), or is it better to risk saying there is no difference when the experimental group is really better (a Type II error)?

Since statistically significant results seem to be regarded as a research "finding" more often than insignificant results, Type I errors are more likely to find their way into print.

References

Anderson, Scarvia, et. al. Encyclopedia of Educational Evaluation. San Francisco: Jossey-Bass, 1975.

Fitz-Gibbon, Carol, and Lynn Morris. How To Calculate Statistics. University of California at Los Angeles Center for the Study of Evaluation. Beverly Hills, Calif.: Sage Publications.

This lesson is reprinted from the August 1983 issue of How To Evaluate Education Programs.

NOTES

Lesson 9

How To Compare Programs And Participants

As more and more states and school districts adopt various education reform proposals, evaluators will be expected to come up with sound plans for comparing their results.

Evaluation designs fall roughly into two categories: experimental and nonexperimental. When you assign students to a particular program and then analyze the results, you are using an experimental design.

When you simply observe and analyze a regular classroom or compare existing programs, you are using a nonexperimental design. The difference lies in your ability to control or manipulate people and events.

Experimental designs are better than nonexperimental designs if you want to prove that a program works. Nonexperimental designs are not good at establishing causal relationships. Remember that the integrity of any design depends on how well it meets certain criteria for internal and external validity.

Internal validity means you can distinguish between changes caused by the program and those that result from outside events. External validity refers to the likelihood that your evaluation findings will hold true if the program is tried in other places with other people.

To help you visualize different evaluation designs, we're going to use a form of notation used by many evaluators to describe their designs. Observations or measurements are represented by O's, and the programs being evaluated (the independent variables) are X's.

For example, if one group participates in a program and you observe the group once before the program and twice after, you would diagram it like this:

$O_1 \ X \ O_2 \ O_3$.

Two groups in different programs who are observed at the same times would be represented this way: $O_1 \ X_1 \ O_2 \ O_3$
$O_1 \ X_2 \ O_2 \ O_3$.

Let's start with one-group designs. Many of these will be familiar to you, although they're not considered experimental. People are not usually assigned to groups or programs--you just take them as they are and study them in different ways.

The Pretest-Posttest Design

This is a time series design with two measurements of the dependent variable, one before the program and one after. It looks like this: $O_1 \ X \ O_2$.

This is an easy design to use, because participants in the program serve as their own control, and comparisons are made before and after participation. But beware of threats to validity, such as the effects of testing, or the Hawthorne effect, or even some change in the environment that took place about the same time as the program.

Example: The evaluators of a program aimed at teaching children to take better care of their health asked, "Did the children who participated in the program assume more responsibility for their own health care than they had before?" They selected a pretest-posttest design, measuring the children immediately before the program started and again immediately after it ended.

The Interrupted Time Series

The design is similar to the pretest-posttest, but there are more than two measurements. Here are some variations:

$O_1 \ O_2 \ O_3 \ O_4 \ X \ O_5 \ O_6 \ O_7 \ O_8$;

$O_1 \ X \ O_2 \ O_3$; and

$O_1 \ O_2 \ldots\ldots\ldots\ldots O_{50} \ X \ O_{51} \ O_{52} \ldots\ldots\ldots\ldots O_{100}$.

The advantage of the interrupted time series is that it allows you to monitor trends over time and to see the direction in which things were going before the program was introduced. If reading scores were going up at a certain rate before the new program started, for example, this design could tell you whether the program speeded up the rate of improvement, slowed it down, or left it climbing at the same rate as before.

Don't try this design unless you are capable of fairly sophisticated analysis techniques, and take special precautions against variations in test administration or other instrumentation errors.

Example: In a program to raise the self-concept of disadvantaged first-graders, evaluators asked: "Did the improvements in self-concept noted at the end of the program hold up over time?" They chose an interrupted time series design, measuring the students' self-concept twice before the program (once in kindergarten and once at the beginning of the first grade) and three times after the program (immediately after, at the end of second grade and at the end of third grade).

Correlational Designs

These are sometimes called case designs, and the evaluator doesn't intervene in any way. Measurements such as observations, surveys, or record reviews are collected from a group and used to describe the program. This approach is often used with innovative programs such as alternative schools.

In a <u>cross-sectional design</u>, all measurements are taken at the same time: O. This design is simple and inexpensive, since it requires nothing more than collecting two or more measures. It may be the only design possible in certain settings. With it, you can determine whether two variables are related. For more than two variables, you will have to turn to more sophisticated techniques like regression.

<u>Example</u>: To answer the question, "What is the relationship between a student's enjoyment of reading and his or her reading achievement in program C?" the evaluator compared scores on the Attitude Toward Reading Inventory with scores on the Program C Reading Achievement Test.

<u>Longitudinal designs</u> are a variation of the correlational design and require two or more measurements on the same group: $O_1\ O_2 \ldots\ldots\ldots O_{10}$.

Measurements can go on over long periods of time, and more than two variables can be studied. Like the time series, this design calls for sophisticated analysis and special precautions against instrumentation errors.

<u>Example</u>: To gauge the success of its high school vocational program, the district asked, "Did the salaries of students who graduated from the program keep pace with inflation?" The evaluator collected information about income from students one year, three years and five years after graduation.

Multiple Or Comparison Group Designs

Designs that involve <u>comparisons of two or more groups in different programs</u> are experimental. When the groups or the programs are randomly assigned, the designs are termed "true experimental." With nonrandom assignment, they are called "quasi-experimental."

A two-group design is the simplest of the experimental designs, with one independent and one dependent variable: $X_1\ O_1$
$X_2\ O_1$.

The X's represent the two programs, while the O's are measures or observations of the dependent variable. With this design, the evaluator assigns participants to programs and then observes the consequences.

If random assignment is used it may be possible to conclude that differences in performance at O_1 are due to the program. But random assignment is not always possible, and without it, you can't be sure that differences in performance are due to the program and not to some inherent difference in the participating groups.

Example A: Students were allowed to choose between the district's traditional Spanish-language program and a new "total immersion" approach. At the end of the first year, evaluators compared the Spanish-speaking ability of participants in the two programs.

Example B: Evaluators randomly assigned students to two different Spanish-language programs in an attempt to find out which program was the more effective. At the end of the first year, evaluators compared the Spanish-speaking ability of participants in the two programs.

With a multiple-group posttest design you can compare a number of different programs (independent variables) on a single dependent variable measured once. The design looks like this:
$$X_1\ O_1$$
$$X_2\ O_1$$
$$*$$
$$*$$
$$*$$
$$X_n\ O_1.$$

This has the advantage of providing several controls—for example, new program A compared to the traditional program B compared to another school's programs C and D. But it's expensive to monitor because of the number of programs and people it involves.

Example: To find out if students in the new physics program in School A are progressing satisfactorily, evaluators compared their scores on an achievement test of physics knowledge at the end of the school year to scores of students in the school's traditional program and scores of students in two other innovative programs in the state.

If you add pretest observations to the example above, you then have a multiple-group pretest-posttest design like this:
$$O_1\ X_1\ O_2$$
$$O_1\ X_2\ O_2$$
$$*$$
$$*$$
$$*$$
$$O_1\ X_n\ O_2.$$

The advantage of this design is that you can demonstrate the level of performance associated with the dependent variable before and after the program. This is important when you want to show that the groups were alike in all important respects before the program.

It also provides a baseline against which to compare effects when you can't come up with a control group that has had no program at all. This design is used frequently by evaluators precisely because it is difficult to get the untreated control you should have to show what might have happened to participants if they had been left alone.

Example: To find out how much student performance improved in a six-week music course, students in Programs X, Y and Z were tested before entry into their respective courses and immediately after.

If you add more measurements or observations to the previous design, it becomes a <u>multiple-group time series</u>. A two-group, four-measurement design could be diagrammed as: $O_1\ O_2\ X_1\ O_3\ O_4$
$O_1\ O_2\ X_2\ O_3\ O_4.$

Evaluators like this design (especially with random assignment) because it provides comparison groups and enables you to spot trends taken by the dependent variables before and after the program.

Example: Programs A and B for children with certain learning disorders cost about the same and both require six months to complete. An evaluation was commissioned to find out which one provided the better learning experience. To answer this question, the evaluator selected a design in which the achievement test scores of children in both programs were compared six months before they entered the program, immediately before, at the end, and six months later.

Factorial Designs

Some experimental designs have several independent variables. To simplify analysis, these are usually placed in a factorial structure. One of the simplest is the <u>2 x 2 factorial design</u>.

This design consists of two independent variables with two levels in each. For example, if the independent variables are sex (male vs. female) and program (A vs. B), the design would have four treatment combinations or cells: males receiving program A, males receiving program B, females with A and females with B:

	Sex	
Program	Male	Female
A		
B		

These designs make it possible for you to determine the joint effects of the independent variables (interactions) as well as their separate or main effects.

A <u>main effect</u> in a factorial design is the independent effect of one particular variable, such as program or sex. To find the main effects, you could compare all males with all females regardless of which program they were in, or you could compare participants in program A with those in program B regardless of their sex.

The joint effect, or interaction, takes both variables into account. When you are looking for interactions, you want to answer questions like this: "Are differences between program A and program B the same for males as for females?"

What you need to know is whether males and females show the same pattern--both going up or both going down, for example--not whether one scores higher or lower than the other.

The following illustrations show several possible combinations of main effects and interactions. For each graph, the x-axis represents the independent variable, program, which has two values, A and B. The y-axis represents the dependent variable, reading, and the two lines labeled male and female represent the independent variable, sex.

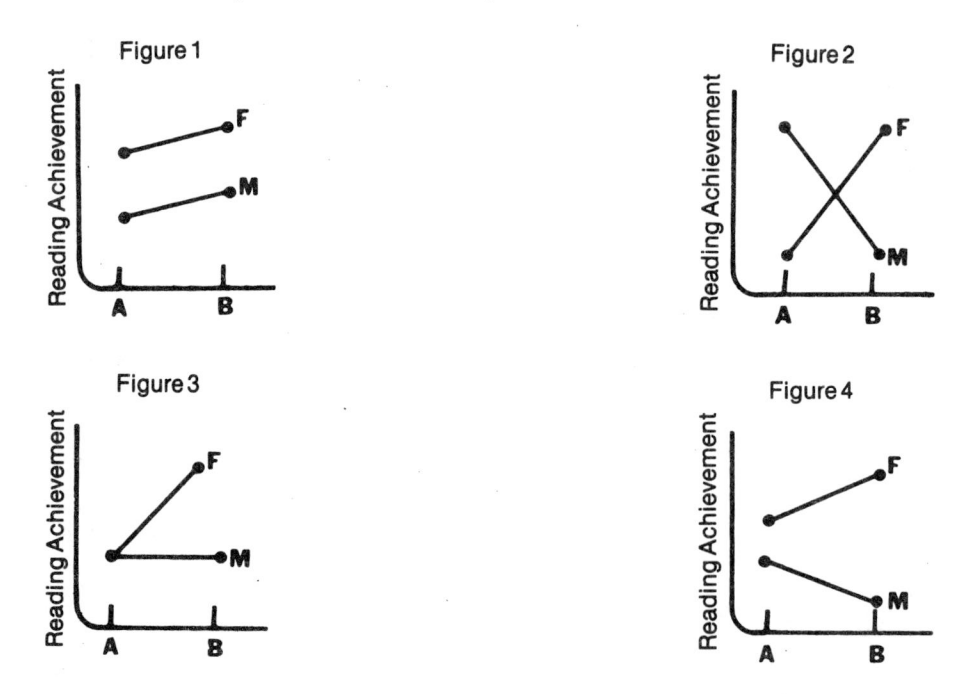

Figure 1 indicates two main effects and no interaction. Females are higher than males for both programs, and program B is higher than program A for both sexes. The two parallel lines show the pattern of results is the same for both sexes, so there is no interaction.

Figure 2 shows a case of interaction with no main effects. The pattern for males and females is exactly opposite--males are higher on A than B, and females are higher on B and A. Overall, neither program is higher than the other and neither sex is higher than the other. The interaction is shown by the "x" pattern formed by the two lines.

Figure 3 and 4 illustrate two other possible interactions. Figure 3 shows no difference on the program variable for males, but there is a difference for females. Furthermore, females and males do not differ on A, only on B. In Figure 4, females are higher than males for both programs but show an opposite pattern. While females are higher on B than A, males are higher on A than B. This pattern is similar to Figure 2 except that there is now a main effect for sex.

Interactions are more precise statements of the results than main effects. Once you find an interaction, you should probably discard the main effects. This is especially true with patterns like the one in Figure 3, where a difference is found only for females.

If you combine the 2 x 2 factorial and the pretest-posttest designs, you have what is called the Solomon four-group design. Its main virtue is that it helps to guard against the reactive effects of testing, when the use of pretests can raise scores on the posttest.

It is similar to the factorial designs because people are assigned to a 2 x 2 grid, and similar to the pretest-posttest because they are measured twice. In this case, however, only half get the pretest: $O_1 \ X_1 \ O_2$

$$X_1 \ O_2$$
$$O_1 \ X_2 \ O_2$$
$$X_2 \ O_2.$$

With this design you can compare people whose only presumed difference is that some have been given a pretest, and you can assess the extent of change over time for each treatment. The main disadvantage of this design is the potential complexity of the data analysis.

Example: An evaluation of an experimental math program asked whether students showed a significant improvement in their ability to reason mathematically, and how they compared to other math students. To answer these questions, the evaluator compared students in the experimental program with students in the traditional. Only half the students in either program got a pretest, but all students were given a posttest.

Other Designs And Variations

1. MXN Factorial Design. The 2 x 2 design can be expanded to include all levels of an independent variable, within practical limits. For example, you might be interested in three programs and four counties--two independent variables in a 3 x 4 design.

2. Higher Order Factorial Design. In some cases you may want to assess more than two independent variables. For example, you may want to know how boys (independent variable 1) from four different backgrounds (independent variable 2) who participate in one of six programs (independent variable 3) compare with girls of differing backgrounds in one of the six programs. As the number of independent variables increases, so does the need for a sample large enough to fill all the cells. A 2 x 2 design has four cells, but a 2 x 2 x 2 x 2 has 16, requiring four times as many participants.

3. Multivariate Designs. These designs have several dependent variables. Their supporters argue that program effects are rarely confined to a single variable. Although computers have made it possible to use these more often, their complexity has limited their application to relatively large programs.

4. <u>Ex Post Facto Designs</u>. In these retrospective studies, the evaluator steps back in time to try to uncover the reason for certain conditions. Suppose you have two groups of students and one performs much better in arithmetic than the other. One way to find the reason for the difference would be to "match" students according to factors like age, sex or family background. If a difference remains after controlling for all reasonable factors except participation in a particular program, you might conclude that the program was responsible. This design has fallen into disfavor because it is so difficult to account for all the variables that make people and groups different from one another.

References

Spector, Paul E. <u>Research Design</u>. Beverly Hills, Calif.: Sage Publications, 1981.

Campbell, D.T., and J.C. Stanley. <u>Experimental and Quasi-Experimental Designs for Research</u>. Chicago: Rand McNally, 1966.

This lesson is reprinted from the June 1985 issue of How To Evaluate Education Programs.

NOTES

Lesson 10

How To Use Pattern Analysis

Did you ever have to choose between two pints of strawberries at the supermarket? Either one pint is clearly better and the choice is easy, or they look about the same. Then you can either count the green and the rotten strawberries in each pint--or, more likely, squint your eyes and pick the pint that is the reddest overall. Evaluators often face the same problems--only on a much larger scale.

Large evaluation projects usually involve data from many different measures. A statewide evaluation of the comparative merit of two compensatory education programs, for example, might use reading comprehension, vocabulary, arithmetic and social studies tests. How can you interpret all this information and decide on the merit of each program? One way is to find statistically significant results consistently favoring one of the two programs. A less reliable, but still acceptable procedure is to find whether most of the differences favor one program--to squint your eyes, so to speak--and then see if this "pattern of differences" is itself statistically significant. This is called pattern analysis.

RZA: A Hypothetical Case Study

The RZA research firm conducted a statewide evaluation of two vocational education programs, each of which sought to help students enter the job market. Program A, a new program, emphasized eliminating sex biases and expanding students' career horizons; program B offered the traditional job training curriculum. RZA had to answer three evaluation questions:

▶ Is program A better than program B in improving students' cognitive skills?

▶ Is program A better than program B in enhancing students' work-related activities?

▶ Is program A better than program B in promoting positive attitudes and values in students?

In the course of RZA's evaluation, students entering vocational education programs in the state's high schools were randomly assigned to the new or old program. In 1976, when students were in the 12th grade, and again in 1980, RZA put each participant through a complete battery of tests of cognitive skills, work-related activities, and attitudes and values. Each of the tests had several subscales.

The basic design for the evaluation was a time-series in which males and females were separately tracked--primarily because they often participated in classes predominantly of one sex. The design looked like this:

	Females		Males	
	1976	1980	1976	1980

After successfully administering all the measures and getting a 98% response rate in all groups, the RZA evaluators began to analyze the 20 different measures (the cognitive skills and the work-related activities test batteries each had eight subscales and the attitudes and values battery had four). When the evaluators compared program A with program B across all the measures in each group (1976 females, 1980 females, 1976 males and 1980 males) they found very few statistically significant results--although in most cases program A seemed to work better than program B. Since neither program could meet the criterion of consistent statistically significant differences for each measure, RZA decided to conduct a pattern analysis.

Terms And Tables

Single Group Differences: Again, the evaluators had four groups for which they could compare any single measure used in program A (the new course) and program B (the traditional course). For the pattern analysis, RZA used summary tables to show the "direction" of single group score differences, rather than to give means and standard deviations. "Direction" was represented by A>B, B>A, or A=B. This way of presenting findings was less time-consuming and also was intuitively meaningful. In addition to showing the differences, RZA's summary tables also showed, with asterisks, whether each difference was statistically significant at the .05 and .01 levels of confidence. For example, a typical table might look like this:

Sample Table

Measure	1976 Females		1980 Females		1976 Males		1980 Males	
	Direction of Difference	Significance	Direction of Difference	Significance	Direction of Difference	Significance	Direction of Difference	Significance
Composite score	A > B	**	A = B		A > B		A > B	*
Score x	A = B		B > A		A > B		A = B	
Score y	A > B		A = B		A = B		A = B	

* $p < .05$ ** $p < .01$

Trends: For each of the 20 measures, the evaluators computed differences for each of the four groups (1976 females, 1980 females, 1976 males and 1980 males). The evaluators defined a "trend" as follows:

- At least three of four groups must show the same direction (i.e., at least three of the single differences show A>B, or three show B>A; or

- Two groups have the same direction and the other groups do not show the opposite direction (i.e., at least two of the single differences show A>B, or two show B>A, and the others show A=B); or

- One group shows statistically significant differences and none of the other groups shows the opposite (i.e., at least one of the single group differences show A>B or B>A, this difference is statistically significant at p<.05 or p<.01, and the other differences show A=B).

In the sample table, there was one trend supporting program A (composite score).

The Sign Test*

The sign test gets its name from its use of plus and minus signs rather than quantitative metrics. In RZA's evaluation, the evaluators used a plus sign whenever A>B and a minus sign whenever A<B. No signs are assigned to ties.

The null hypothesis tested by the sign test is that the number of plus signs is equal to the number of minus signs. That is, the sign test assesses whether A>B as often as A<B. The null hypothesis is rejected when too few differences of one sign occur.

There are statistical tables for interpreting sign test data. To use them you need to know only the total number of plus and minus signs (called by statisticians N), and the number of minus signs (called by statisticians x). The columns of the table are arranged by increasing N's, and the rows by increasing x's. For any given N and x, the entries of the table give the probability, or p-value. For example, if N=14 and x=5, a sign test table show will p=.212. This p-value is not significant at p<.05.

But very few statistics texts give a sign table. Fortunately, computing the p-value is not too difficult, and you can do it with a hand calculator. The probability of having a certain number of pluses and minuses is based on a mathematical concept called binomial distribution. The sign test assumes that the probability of getting a plus or a minus is equal. In this situation, the formula for the binomial distribution can be written as follows:

$$\binom{N}{x}\left(\frac{1}{2}\right)^N = \frac{N!}{x!\,(N-x)!}\left(\frac{1}{2}\right)^N$$

Consider the evaluation question on work-related activities. Evaluators could make 32 single group comparisons between programs A and B (eight measures times four groups). RZA found that out of 32 comparisons, 20 favored program A (20 pluses), four favored program B (four minuses), and eight

---

*The sign test described here is for a situation where there are fewer than 30 single group differences or matched pairs.

were ties. They then tested the null hypothesis that the number of pluses and minuses were equal, and the alternative hypothesis was that there were more pluses. In this case, N=24 (the ties are not counted) and x=4, and the binomial formula $\binom{24}{4}(\frac{1}{2})^{24}$--or a table--gives p=.001 (a significant result). RZA therefore rejected the null hypothesis and suggested that the pattern of differences significantly favored program A.

RZA's Findings

<u>Is program A better than program B in improving students' cognitive skills?</u>

The evaluators had information from eight measures of cognitive skills: reading, writing, vocabulary, abstract reasoning, science, social science, mathematics and a composite score.

Overall, students in program A scored better in cognitive skills than did students in program B. In the 32 possible comparisons between the groups, program A students scored higher in 25 cases, lower in three cases, and the same in four cases (see Table 1).

Table 1: Cognitive Skills

Measure	1976 Females		1980 Females		1976 Males		1980 Males	
	Direction of Difference	Significance	Direction of Difference	Significance	Direction of Difference	Significance	Direction of Difference	Significance
Composite score	A > B	**	A > B		A > B		A > B	
Reading	A > B	**	A > B		A > B		A > B	
Writing	A > B		A > B		B > A		A > B	
Vocabulary	A > B	*	A > B		A > B		A > B	
Abstract reasoning	A > B		B > A		A = B		A > B	
Science	A > B		A = B		A = B		A > B	
Social science	A > B		A = B		B > A		A > B	
Mathematics	A > B	*	A > B		A > B		A > B	

* p < .05   ** p < .01

The evaluators found trends favoring program A in all measures except social science and abstract reasoning. Only four of the differences were statistically significant: 1976 program A females scored significantly better than did program B females in reading, vocabulary, mathematics and composite scores.

To test the significance of the pattern of differences--which seemed to favor program A, even though most differences were not statistically significant--the evaluators computed a sign test, which showed students in program A did indeed perform significantly better than those in program B (p<.01).

Is program A better than program B in enhancing students' work-related activities?

There were eight measures of work-related activities: adjusted hourly earnings, hours working for pay each week, definiteness of occupational plans, expected earnings at 40 years of age, job satisfaction, number of household chores performed, employer satisfaction, and a composite score (see Table 2).

Once again, the evaluators found new significant single group differences between programs, but many patterns. Out of 32 tests, 20 differences favored programs A, and this overall trend was proved significant by the sign test ($p<.01$).

Table 2: Work-Related Activities

Measure	1976 Females Direction of Difference	Significance	1980 Females Direction of Difference	Significance	1976 Males Direction of Difference	Significance	1980 Males Direction of Difference	Significance
Composite score	A > B		A = B		A > B		A > B	
Adjusted hourly earnings	A > B		A > B		A > B	*	A > B	*
Hours worked for pay each week	A = B		A = B		A = B		A = B	
Definitions of occupational plans	A > B		A > B		A > B		A > B	
Expected earnings at 40 years of age	A > B	**	A > B		A > B	**	A > B	
Job satisfaction	A > B		B > A		A = B		B > A	
Number of household chores performed	A > B		A > B		A > B		A = B	
Employer satisfaction	A = B		B > A		B > A		A > B	

* $p < .05$ ** $p < .01$

In all, the evaluators found five trends. Students in program A had higher adjusted earnings, more definite occupational plans, higher expected earnings, performed more household chores, and had higher composite scores. The evaluators found four statistically significant single group differences that favored program A.

All these differences related to two measures:

▶ Adjusted hourly earnings (1976 and 1980 program A males had significantly higher earnings).

▶ Expected earnings at 40 years of age (1976 program A males and females had higher expected earnings).

Is program A better than program B in promoting attitudes and values?

RZA studied four measures of attitudes and values: plans for future education, community involvement, self-esteem, and a composite score. The evaluation findings suggested little difference in attitudes and values between students in the two programs (see Table 3).

Table 3: Attitudes and Values

Measure	1976 Females		1980 Females		1976 Males		1980 Males	
	Direction of Difference	Significance	Direction of Difference	Significance	Direction of Difference	Significance	Direction of Difference	Significance
Composite score	A > B	*	A = B		A = B		A > B	
Plans for future education	B > A		A = B		B > A	*	B > A	**
Community involvement	A > B		A = B		B > A		B > A	
Self-esteem	A = B		A > B		B > A		A > B	

* $p < .05$ ** $p < .01$

On the 16 possible differences (four measures times four groups), students in program A scored higher in five cases, lower in six cases, and the same in five cases. There are two trends in the table, but they are in opposite directions, and a sign test showed that the overall pattern of differences was not significant. The only <u>subpattern</u> the evalutors could discern in table 3 was a <u>tendency</u> for program B males to report more positive attitudes and values than their program A counterparts in 1976. This tendency is a vertical subpattern—not a trend—that encompasses all four measures of attitudes and values.

References

Claudy, John G., et. al. "The Consequences of Being an Only Child: An Analysis of Project Talent Data." American Institutes for Research, AIR-75501-12/79-FR. Palo Alto, Calif.: Dec. 1979.

Siegal, Sidney. <u>Nonparametric Statistics for the Behavioral Sciences</u>. New York: McGraw Hill, 1956.

This lesson is reprinted from the October 1984 issue of
How To Evaluate Education Programs.

NOTES

Lesson 11

How To Measure Teaching Performance

Although most colleges and universities consider teaching important, good teachers are not always the ones who get ahead. When it comes to promotions, criteria other than teaching ability often take precedence.

Frequently, the people with the most publications or those with a record of community or university service advance more quickly than good teachers.

Many have tried to explain why teaching is not highly rated. One obvious reason is that it's difficult to measure teaching effectiveness. Those who advocate promoting the best teachers are unable to define what they mean.

In this lesson, we will summarize a study that involved more than 1,600 college students and faculty in an effort to describe good teaching performance. The guidelines that emerged from that study may help you develop a teacher evaluation plan for your school or college.

Collecting the Data

For two consecutive years, researchers distributed questionnaires to students and faculty at the University of California, Berkeley.

▶ The first questionnaire went to students. It asked for biographical information and included questions about college goals and what the students valued in teaching. It asked them to identify the best and worst instructors they had the previous year, promising confidentiality.

It included a list of 158 descriptions of teaching characteristics such as "speaks clearly," "discusses practical applications," and so on. It asked the students if each item could be used to describe the instructors they called their best and worst teachers.

Some 278 undergraduates and 60 graduates responded, comprising 4% of the student body and 38% of those randomly selected for the survey.

These respondents were typical of Berkeley students overall. They represented different class levels and majors, and about half were women. Their mean grade point average was almost identical to that of the student population.

The second questionnaire was distributed to faculty. It asked them to choose a best and worst teacher among their colleagues and to answer questions about their teaching activities.

This questionnaire was returned by 119 of the faculty members, representing 54% of the random sample and 21% of the resident teaching faculty.

▶ The third questionnaire asked faculty members how they allocated their time among various academic pursuits. It was returned by 162 members of the faculty who had not been asked to complete the previous questionnaire. These respondents accounted for 80% of the random sample and 29% of the resident teaching faculty.

▶ Finally, as a followup and validation study in the second year of the project, the researchers distributed a fourth questionnaire to all students in 51 classes.

Some were classes of instructors who had been identified as best teachers, some were classes of those identified as worst teachers, and some were classes of instructors who had not turned up in either category.

The 1,015 respondents answered questions about their college goals, teaching values and the teaching of the given instructor. They also rated the teacher's overall effectiveness.

Good Teachers, As Seen By Their Students

Students who responded to the first year's survey looked at a list of 158 brief descriptions of teaching behavior, indicating if their best and worst teachers fit each description. Possible answers were "yes," "no," "does not apply," and "don't know."

The second year's survey used most of the same items and added a few new ones. This time, students rated their best and worst teachers on each item by using a four-point scale ranging from "not at all descriptive" to "very descriptive."

Based on the students' assessments of their teachers, the researchers found 85 of the 158 items could be used to distinguish good teachers from bad ones. These items discriminated at the very high significance level of $p<.001$.

How Students Characterized Their Teachers

The symbol * is used to designate items that students said described at least 75 percent of their best teachers and no more than 25 percent of their worst teachers. The symbol + marks items that students said described at least 95 percent of their best teachers and no more than 45 percent of their worst teachers.

Course Content and Presentation

+ * 1. Contrasts implications of various theories
    2. Presents origins of ideas and concepts
    3. Presents facts and concepts from related fields
    4. Talks about research he or she has done himself or herself
    5. Emphasizes ways of solving problems rather than solutions
    6. Discusses practical applications
    7. Explains his or her actions, decisions and selection of topics
+   8. Seems well read beyond the subject taught
*   9. Is an excellent public speaker

How Students Characterized Their Teachers (Cont.)

+ 10. Speaks clearly
* 11. Explains clearly
  12. Gives lectures that are easy to outline
  13. Reads lectures or stays close to notes (Negative)
  14. Assigns test, but lectures include other topics
* 15. Makes difficult topics easy to understand
  16. Summarizes major points
  17. States objectives for each class session
  18. Identifies what he or she considers important
* 19. Shows interest and concern in quality of teaching
  20. Gives examinations requiring creative, original thinking
  21. Gives examinations having instructional value
  22. Gives examinations requiring chiefly recall of facts (Negative)
  23. Gives interesting and stimulating assignments
  24. Stresses the aesthetic and emotional value of the subject
* 25. Is a dynamic and energetic person
+ * 26. Seems to enjoy teaching
+ 27. Is enthusiastic about subject
  28. Seems to have self-confidence
  29. Varies the speed and tone of his or her voice
  30. Has a sense of humor

Relations with Students

  31. Is careful and precise in answering questions
+ 32. Explains own criticisms
  33. Encourages class discussion
* 34. Invites students to share their knowledge and experiences
+ 35. Clarifies thinking by identifying reasons for questions
* 36. Invites criticism of his or her own ideas
+ * 37. Knows if the class is understanding what is being taught
  38. Knows when students are bored or confused
  39. Has students apply concepts to demonstrate understanding
+ * 40. Keeps well informed about progress of class
  41. Anticipates difficulties and prepares students beforehand
  42. Has definite plan, yet uses material introduced by students
  43. Provides time for discussion and questions
  44. Is sensitive to student's desire to ask a question
  45. Encourages students to speak out in lecture or discussion
+ 46. Quickly grasps what a student is asking or stating
  47. Restates questions or comments to clarify for entire class
  48. Asks others to comment on one student's contribution
  49. Compliments students for raising good points
  50. Doesn't fully answer questions (Negative)
  51. Determines if one student's problem is common to others
  52. Reminds students to see him or her if students are having difficulty
  53. Informs students of coming campus events related to course
  54. Encourages students to express feelings and opinions
  55. Relates class topics to students' lives and experiences
+ 56. Has a genuine interest in students
  57. Relates to students as individuals
  58. Recognizes and greets students out of class
* 59. Is valued for advice not directly related to the course
  60. Treats students as equals

Characteristics of a Majority of Best and Worst Teachers, But More Typical of Best

  61. Discusses points of view other than his or her own
  62. Discusses recent developments in the field
  63. Gives references for the most interesting and involved points
  64. Emphasizes conceptual understanding
  65. Disagrees with some ideas in textbook and other readings
  66. Stresses rational and intellectual aspects of the subject
  67. Stresses general concepts and ideas
  68. Seems to have a serious commitment to his or her field
  69. Is well prepared
  70. Gives examinations stressing conceptual understanding
  71. Gives examinations requiring synthesis of various parts of course
  72. Gives examinations permitting students to show understanding
  73. Is friendly toward students
  74. Is accessible to students out of class
  75. Respects students as persons
  76. Is always courteous to students
  77. Gives personal help to students having difficulty with course
  78. Has an interesting style of presentation

How Students Characterized Their Teachers (Cont.)

Results Typical of Taking a Course from a Best Teacher and Not from a Worst Teacher

+ * 79. Have developed increased appreciation for the subject
+ * 80. Have learned new ways to evaluate problems
    81. Have worked harder than in most other courses
    82. Know how to find more information on the subject
    83. Have studied a topic from the course on own initiative
    84. Plan to take more courses on the subject
    85. Have gained self-knowledge

Good Teachers, As Seen By Their Colleagues

Each of the 119 faculty members who responded to the second questionnaire picked a "most effective" and a "least effective" teacher from among their colleagues. These respondents scanned a list of 103 items describing teaching and other academic activities, noting if each item was characteristic of the teachers they had named. Answers were "yes," "no," "does not apply," and "don't know."

From the 103 original items, 54 were found to discriminate between best and worst teachers with a significance level of $p<.001$.

How Faculty Characterized Their Colleagues

The symbol * is used to show items that faculty members said described 25 percent or more of the best teachers and 25 per cent or less of the worst teachers. The symbol + marks items that faculty members said described 95 percent or more of the best teachers and 45 percent or less of the worst teachers.

Characteristics of a Majority of Best Teachers and a Minority of Worst

    1. Does original and creative work
    2. Expresses interest in the research of colleagues
    3. Gives many papers at conferences
    4. Has done work to which I refer in teaching
    5. Has been consulted by me about by research
    6. Has been consulted by me about problems in his or her field
    7. Discusses students' work with colleagues
+   8. Spends much time planning and preparing for teaching
*   9. Seems well read beyond the subject taught
    10. Is sought by others for advice on research
+ 11. Can suggest reading in any area of his or her general field
    12. Is sought by colleagues for advice on academic matters
    13. Encourages students to discuss matters of concern
    14. Is involved in campus activities that affect students
    15. Attends many lectures and other events on campus
    16. Enjoys controversy in discussion and may provoke opposing views
+ 17. Comes to departmental or committee meetings well prepared
    18. Meets with students informally out of class
    19. Meets with students out of regular office hours
    20. Encourages students to talk with him or her
+ 21. Discusses teaching in general with colleagues
+ 22. Seems to have a genuine interest in his or her students

How Faculty Characterized Their Colleagues (Cont.)

* 23. Seeks advice from others about the courses he or she teaches
+ 24. Discusses teaching with colleagues
   25. Does not seek close friendships with colleagues (Negative)
   26. Is someone with whom I have discussed my teaching
   27. Is interested in, and informed about, the work of colleagues
   28. Expresses interest and concern about the quality of his or her teaching
+ 29. Seems to enjoy teaching

Further Characterization if Speech or Seminar was Attended

+ 30. Gives a well-organized presentation
* 31. Is an excellent public speaker
   32. Summarizes major points at the end of the presentation
* 33. Uses wit and humor effectively
+ 34. Uses well-chosen examples to clarify points
+ 35. Communicates self-confidence

Further Characterization if Classroom Teaching was Observed

   36. Encourages students to express feelings and opinions
* 37. Clarifies thinking by identifying reasons for questions
   38. Presents facts and concepts from related fields

* 39. Anticipates difficulties and prepares students beforehand
+ 40. Quickly grasps what a student is asking or stating
+ 41. Is careful and precise in answering questions
   42. Presents origins of ideas and concepts
+ 43. Emphasizes ways of solving problems rather than solutions

Characteristics of a Majority of Best and Worst Teachers, But More Typical of Best

44. Invites discussion of points he or she raises
45. Is careful and precise in answering questions
46. Keeps current with developments in field
47. Has talked with me about his or her research
48. Knows about developments in fields other than own
49. Has a congenial relationship with colleagues
50. Is conscientious about keeping appointments with students
51. Recognizes and greets students out of class
52. Is enthusiastic about subject
53. Does work that receives serious attention from others
54. Corresponds with others about his or her research

How To Shorten The Evaluation Form

By sorting individual items into related groups, many researchers have come up with basic components, dimensions or scales of effective teaching. This can be done by examining the groups subjectively or by using factor analysis, which mathematically establishes the tendency of responses to various items to associate in clusters.

In the Berkeley study, a statistical analysis yielded a number of components, but four appeared consistently. They were: knowledge, presentations, relations with students, and enthusiasm.

An analysis of the 85 items students said characterized best teachers produced five scales or components of effective performance:

1. Analytic/synthetic approach
2. Organization/clarity
3. Instructor-group interaction
4. Instructor-individual student interaction
5. Dynamism/enthusiasm

An analysis of the 54 items that faculty respondents named as characteristic of best teachers among their colleagues produced five scales:

1. Research activity and recognition
2. Intellectual breadth
3. Participation in the academic community
4. Relations with students
5. Concern for teaching

Using data from students and faculty, the Berkeley researchers prepared a shortened evaluation form. They recommend using a seven-point scale with it, ranging from "not at all descriptive" to "very descriptive."

The shortened version of the evaluation form:

1. Has command of the subject, presents material in an analytical way, contrasts various points of view, discusses current developments and relates topics to other areas of knowledge.

2. Makes himself or herself clear, states objectives, summarizes major points, presents material in an organized manner and provides emphasis.

3. Is sensitive to the response of the class, encourages student participation and welcomes questions and discussion.

4. Is available and friendly toward students, is interested in students as individuals, is respected as a person and is valued for advice not directly related to the course.

5. Enjoys teaching, is enthusiastic about the subject, makes the course exciting and has self-confidence.

Getting Started On A Successful Teacher Evaluation System

Try the following checklist to help you get started on an evaluation program tailored to your own school and faculty.

Evaluation Checklist

What is the purpose of this evaluation?
  Give feedback to instructor for self-improvement
  Gather data for making salary, promotion and tenure decisions
  Collect information to assist students in choosing courses and instructors
  A combination of the above

What is the scope of this evaluation?
  Number of Teachers
    Small number (e.g., all in one department)
    Medium number (e.g., all eligible for tenure)
    Large number (e.g., all in the institution)
  Number of classes
    One per instructor per advancement period
    One per instructor per year
    Each once per advancement period
    Each every other year, or every year
  Number of students
    Random sample of X students (large classes only?)
    X percent of class (large classes only?)
    All (but with minimum of X returns to qualify for interpretation?)
  Kinds of courses
    Undergraduate credit courses
    All except seminars and field research courses
    All (including noncredit and extension?)

What forms will be needed?
  Style
    Structured check-off items

Evaluation Checklist (Cont.)

    Open-ended essay items
- Coverage
  - Teaching only
  - Teaching and course
  - Teaching, course and student data (demographic, objectives, values)
- Format
  - Optical scanning sheets
  - Mark sense sheets
  - Porto-punch cards
  - Duplicated questionnaire with key punch
  - Duplicated questionnaire with hand tally
- Length
  - Short (1-25 items)
  - Medium (26-50 items)
  - Long (more than 50 items)
- Sources
  - External (e.g., another campus, Center for Research and Development in Higher Education, Berkeley)
  - Local committee (faculty, administrative, student, combination)
  - Instructor
  - A combination of the above

How will surveys and questionnaires be administered?

- Time of distribution
  - Early in course
  - Late in course
  - With final examination
  - After course
- Method of distribution
  - Instructor
  - Student representative
  - Administrative representative
  - With registration packets
  - Mail
- Method of return
  - Collected by instructor
  - Collected by student representative
  - Collected by administrative representative
  - Mailed to a central office

What is the data reduction plan?

- Persons involved
  - Instructor
  - Department
  - Committee (student, faculty, administrative, combination)
  - Central office
- Method
  - Summarization by computer, with norms and variances
  - Hand-tabulation and individual case study
  - Summarization of open-ended data

How will data be interpreted?

- Persons involved
  - Instructor
  - Department
  - Committee (student, faculty, administrative, combination)
  - Central office
- Basis
  - Individual case study
  - Departmental norms
  - College or school norms
  - Campus norms

Any provision for challenge?

- None
- By instructor
- By students or department

How will results be reported and disseminated?

- To instructor only
- To instructor and departmental chairman or committee
- To instructor, department and administration
- To university community at a central location
- To university community by sale or general distribution

References

Dienst, Evelyn R., et. al. <u>Evaluating University Teaching</u>. Berkeley, Calif.: University of California Center for Research and Development in Higher Education, 1971.

This lesson is reprinted from the November 1985 issue of <u>How To Evaluate Education Programs</u>.

Here is an extra evaluation checklist for you to cut out and use.

Evaluation Checklist

What is the purpose of this evaluation?
- Give feedback to instructor for self-improvement
- Gather data for making salary, promotion and tenure decisions
- Collect information to assist students in choosing courses and instructors
- A combination of the above

What is the scope of this evaluation?
- Number of Teachers
  - Small number (e.g., all in one department)
  - Medium number (e.g., all eligible for tenure)
  - Large number (e.g., all in the institution)
- Number of classes
  - One per instructor per advancement period
  - One per instructor per year
  - Each once per advancement period
  - Each every other year, or every year
- Number of students
  - Random sample of X students (large classes only?)
  - X percent of class (large classes only?)
  - All (but with minimum of X returns to qualify for interpretation?)
- Kinds of courses
  - Undergraduate credit courses
  - All except seminars and field research courses
  - All (including noncredit and extension?)

What forms will be needed?
- Style
  - Structured check-off items
  - Open-ended essay items
- Coverage
  - Teaching only
  - Teaching and course
  - Teaching, course and student data (demographic, objectives, values)
- Format
  - Optical scanning sheets
  - Mark sense sheets
  - Porto-punch cards
  - Duplicated questionnaire with key punch
  - Duplicated questionnaire with hand tally
- Length
  - Short (1-25 items)
  - Medium (26-50 items)
  - Long (more than 50 items)
- Sources
  - External (e.g., another campus, Center for Research and Development in Higher Education, Berkeley)
  - Local committee (faculty, administrative, student, combination)
  - Instructor
  - A combination of the above

How will surveys and questionnaires be administered?
- Time of distribution
  - Early in course
  - Late in course
  - With final examination
  - After course
- Method of distribution
  - Instructor
  - Student representative
  - Administrative representative
  - With registration packets
  - Mail
- Method of return
  - Collected by instructor
  - Collected by student representative
  - Collected by administrative representative
  - Mailed to a central office

What is the data reduction plan?
- Persons involved
  - Instructor
  - Department
  - Committee (student, faculty, administrative, combination)
  - Central office
- Method
  - Summarization by computer, with norms and variances
  - Hand-tabulation and individual case study
  - Summarization of open-ended data

How will data be interpreted?
- Persons involved
  - Instructor
  - Department
  - Committee (student, faculty, administrative, combination)
  - Central office
- Basis
  - Individual case study
  - Departmental norms
  - College or school norms
  - Campus norms

Any provision for challenge?
- None
- By instructor
- By students or department

How will results be reported and disseminated?
- To instructor only
- To instructor and departmental chairman or committee
- To instructor, department and administration
- To university community at a central location
- To university community by sale or general distribution

NOTES

Lesson 12

How To Use A Nominal Group Process To Define Merit

Is your school system considering a merit pay plan for teachers? Here's how one district (we'll call it Lincoln City) tackled the problem of setting criteria for distributing the money. First, a brief overview:

The Lincoln City school board will determine the amount of money to be allocated each year for merit pay. Up to 30% of the teachers in each school will be eligible to receive bonuses of varying amounts, based on criteria to be worked out by a team of teachers, school administrators and parents. Each school will allocate bonuses after a review committee assesses and assigns points for each teacher.

The review process will be the job of the school principal and two teachers (one from another school) who will be elected for two-year terms. The criteria for meritorious performance will be established through "nominal group meetings" of teachers, administrators and parents, chosen by their peers.

Three different teams will hold nominal group meetings, one to set criteria for elementary teachers, one for middle school teachers, and one for high school teachers.

The nominal group process, briefly discussed in an earlier lesson, uses a highly structured meeting that eliminates some of the pressures people usually encounter when they work in a committee.

A relatively quiet person cannot be easily intimidated by more vocal and opinionated members, for example, and a person with unpopular views cannot easily be ignored. A nominal group process gives everyone a chance to express his or her views. Because it's highly structured and depends on a formal set of rules, you should learn as much as possible about how a nominal group meeting works before you try to hold one. Look for additional sources at the end of this lesson.

How To Choose Members Of The Group

Selecting participants for a nominal group meeting is not really part of the formal process since it takes place beforehand. But the better the group you choose, the more successful the meeting is likely to be. Nominal group meetings work best with no more than 10 people.

As a general rule, you will want people who have experience, expertise or insight bearing directly on the problem you want to solve. In the case of a merit pay plan for teachers, a major task is to agree on a definition of merit.

Who can best judge teaching performance? The nominal group chosen to define merit might include teachers, principals, parents, students, employers, members of the school board, union officials and education deans from a local college.

Lincoln City decided to have three meetings—one to define merit for elementary school teachers, one for junior or middle school teachers, and one for senior high teachers. The three committees might look like this:

Nominal Group Committees to Define Meritorious Teaching Performance

Committee #1: Elementary School	Committee #2: Middle School	Committee #3: High School
4 teachers	3 teachers	2 teachers
2 parents	2 parents	parent
school board member	school board member	school board member
principal	principal	principal
union representative	curriculum expert	student
other administrator	education professor	education professor
		local employer
Total 10	9	8

How To Introduce The Nominal Group Procedure

When you explain the purpose of the nominal group meeting (to define merit in teaching, for example), be sure to tell participants that you will be considering both subjective and objective qualities.

Subjective qualities are those that have to do primarily with feelings, such as love of teaching or concern for students, and they are generally hard to measure. Objective qualities can be organizational or environmental—keeps an orderly classroom, gives clear instructions, assigns regular homework, to name a few. Qualities such as these are more easily observed and measured.

Give preprinted "task statement forms" to each member of the group. The form should spell out exactly what the group is expected to do (define merit in teaching), and it should leave a space to list both subjective (personal) qualities and more objective (measurable) ones.

Task Statement Form

How would you define merit in teaching? List the subjective (personal) qualities and the objective (observable) qualities of the best teacher.

Subjective (personal) qualities	Objective (observable) qualities
1. ...	1. ...
2. ...	2. ...
3. ...	3. ...
4. etc.	4. etc.

As leader of the group you should read the task statement aloud and offer some examples of subjective and objective qualities. Don't draw your examples from teaching, as we did above, but from some analogous field such as medicine. Use an illustration like this to start people thinking without influencing their choices:

Example of a completed Task Statement Form

How would you define merit in medical care by a physician? List the subjective (personal) qualities and the objective (observable) qualities of the best doctor.

Subjective (personal) qualities	Objective (observable) qualities
1. Seems to care about patients and listens to what they say.	1. Gets results (e.g., lowers blood pressure, controls diabetes)
2. Reassures patients when they need it.	2. Gives appointments for routine problems (e.g., physical exam) within one week.
3. Doesn't talk down to patients.	3. Never keeps patients waiting more than 15 minutes.

The group can see easily that by replacing "doctor" with "teacher," this form could be used to help define merit for Lincoln City's merit pay plan.

How To Get Started And Keep Going

Give everyone fifteen minutes to write down their own ideas about teaching qualities without consulting each other. No discussion or questions are permitted, and participants should remain seated even if they complete their forms before the fifteen minutes are up. While participants are working, prepare for a brainstorming session with a large pad or flip-chart, masking tape and felt pens.

When the time is up, ask each member of the group in turn to share just one idea, alternating between the subjective and objective columns on the forms. Number each idea consecutively and keep going around the room until you have written and posted all the ideas on every list.

Avoid any debate about overlapping ideas by writing them down exactly as they were stated rather than rewording them to capture differences. Ask participants not to talk out of turn. Discourage discussion, but tell people to write down any new ideas that occur to them and call them out when their turn comes around.

After you've recorded all the ideas, lead the group in discussing them for about 30 minutes. Be sure the ideas are easy to read and everyone can see them. The purpose of the discussion is to clarify, dispute or defend the ideas and to add new ones if they come up. None may be crossed off the list. Keep the talk focused on one idea at a time and never on the list as a whole.

At the end of the discussion, the meeting will have been in progress about an hour. Take a 15 minute break.

How To Decide What's Most Important

When everyone returns, pass out a stack of 3" x 5" cards. Ask each member of the group to choose what they believe are the 10 most important ideas from all those listed and write them (along with their number) on the cards. Use a card for each idea.

After everyone has chosen their top 10, ask them to rank order them by writing "10" on the card with the most important idea, "9" on the card with the second most important idea, and so on. While the group is busy ranking their choices, you can prepare a voting tally sheet on a large flip-chart that looks like this:

Ranking Ideas: Tally Sheet

Idea #	Ranks assigned by participants
1	_____
2	_____
3	_____
4	_____
etc.	_____

As participants complete their rankings, they write the number of points they assigned to each idea on the proper line of the tally sheet. Total the points on each line horizontally. The ranking process usually takes fifteen minutes.

After everyone has recorded his or her vote, give the group a chance to talk it over briefly, so they can defend or challenge this preliminary vote. After a few minutes, ask participants to reconsider and change their choices privately if they want to, reranking the ideas to reflect any changes in their viewpoint.

Again the most important idea gets a score of 10. Participants assign lower scores to the ideas on the other nine cards to reflect their relative importance. It's your job to collect the cards and analyze the results. Here are some of the ways you could report your findings:

1. Idea 10 appeared somewhere on everyone's list of the top ten.

2. Idea 1 received the highest score (82) of all; idea 6 received the second highest (75) ...

3. The top 10 ideas for defining merit are ...

4. Ideas 12, 32, 41 and 60 were chosen by at least half the participants as part of their top ten.

5. No one chose ideas 4, 8 or 12.

6. Ideas 13, 31 and 45 each received a score higher than 75.

7. The average score for idea 1 was ..., for idea 2 it was ...

Pros And Cons For The Nominal Group Process

Most people who participate in the nominal group process like it because it ensures that everyone in the group will have a say. In fact, if you follow the rules, it's almost impossible for any single person to dominate the group or impose his or her views on it.

The process encourages people to be creative, because every idea is considered acceptable and treated seriously. Privacy is another plus, because participants can change their rankings or rate the ideas any way they want to, away from public scrutiny.

Another advantage is that the nominal group meeting is efficient. You can come up with ideas in a few hours that can be used exactly as they are or perhaps offered as preliminary ideas for another group to support or reject.

Critics may say this kind of "efficiency" encourages people to think off the top of their heads just to have something to say when their turn comes. If you decide to try a nominal group meeting, it may be a good idea to ask each member to prepare for it by reading some background material you send beforehand. Any preparation should help to eliminate some frivolous suggestions.

Another drawback you may want to consider is the tendency of all consensus methods to yield ideas that suit everyone only because they aren't very exciting or controversial. And finally, unless you choose members of the group carefully--people who are respected and who represent the interests of important groups--you may find that your conclusions lack credibility. Persuade topnotch people to join the group if you want to get good results.

References

Delbecq, A., and A. Van de Ven. "A Group Process Model for Problem Identification and Program Planning." *Journal of Applied Behavioral Science*, Vol. 7 (1971), pp. 467-492.

Delbecq, A., and A. Van de Ven. "The Nominal Group as a Research Instrument for Exploratory Health Studies." *American Journal of Public Health*, (March 1972), pp. 337-342.

NOTES

Lesson 13

How To Calculate The Costs Of Evaluations

How much did you allow for pain and fear when calculating the costs of your most recent evaluation?

Although these unpleasant sensations are not likely to turn up as line items in your budget, a couple of evaluation experts say you ought to give them serious thought.

The real meaning of cost, says Michael Scriven in a new book (<u>The Costs of Evaluation</u>, edited by Marvin C. Alkin and Lewis C. Solmon for Sage Publications), is "the distastefulness or painfulness involved in acquiring something, or--by no means the same thing--the owned or recognized value given up in order to acquire it."

This notion strikes home to most evaluators, who observe firsthand the pain that any significant change or reform often exacts in our educational system. Minimum competency testing is one example.

As for Scriven's second definition of cost, the "owned or recognized value given up," we can all point to lost opportunities or "foregone alternatives" that we believe might have proved a better investment of scarce funds.

Fear is another aspect of evaluation cost in human terms. Lewis C. Solmon, writing in the same book, contends that "the fear generated by the possibility that evaluation will be used as a mechanism for reducing or withdrawing funds, rather than for improving programs, must be counted as a major cost."

Theorists Solmon and Scriven set the stage for the less philosophical discussions that follow. Scriven, for example, offers some elegant arguments on the finer points of costs in evaluation, but concludes that much of the "technical apparatus" and buzz words of cost analysis are useless to the evaluator.

"Whatever their value to the professional economist or cost analyst in communicating with his or her peers, they offer nothing (as far as I can discover from reading the applied analyses) to the general evaluator, who has little to gain in going beyond the most basic concepts of cost analysis," he writes.

But Scriven holds out for what he calls "cost-free evaluation," not in the sense that you can get it for nothing, but that "any front-end outlay should be recouped by payoffs (benefits) from the results, so that the net cost is negative."

Stalking The Elusive Evaluation Dollar

More interesting to most practicing evaluators is Alkin's report on the results of his survey (with Brian Stecher) to determine how we actually spend our evaluation dollars.

"Our purpose was to explore how the resources used to conduct program evaluation are typically allocated among cost categories. We wanted to establish some general guidelines for evaluation cost and to investigate the effects of selected moderating variables, in order to arrive at a sense of how costs vary and under what conditions these variations arise."

By sticking to the basics of cost analysis, Alkin's study seems to illustrate what Scriven was trying to tell us earlier: cost analysis is important but it doesn't have to be fancy.

"Our general approach was to ask evaluation professionals from a variety of fields to participate in a costing exercise that required them to estimate the costs connected with selected types of evaluation. Assuming that not everyone would agree on the same cost breakdown for a particular evaluation, we also asked respondents to discuss the rationale underlying their estimates. We were interested primarily in learning how much variation there is in evaluation cost breakdowns, which budget categories show the greatest variation, and how the types of evaluation and the size for the total evaluation budget affect cost breakdowns."

Alkin settled for 25 respondents, representing seven school districts, six mental health agencies, three medical schools, two colleges and one social agency. He asked these evaluators to estimate cost breakdowns for two different kinds of evaluations and three different budget levels.

The two types of evaluation were <u>process</u> or <u>implementation</u> (for ongoing programs) and <u>outcome</u> or <u>summative</u> (a typical end-of-year assessment of progress). The three cost levels were set at $25,000, $10,000 and $4,000. Evaluations lasting more than one program year were not included.

The seven cost categories respondents could use were:

- ▶ Professional staff
- ▶ Clerical and secretarial staff
- ▶ External consultants
- ▶ Materials, supplies and telephone
- ▶ Data processing
- ▶ Facilities
- ▶ Travel

Where Does The Money Go?

Well, where does the money go? Just where you thought it would. If you are looking for surprises in Alkin's results, you'll be disappointed. If your own evaluation budgets usually show cost allocations like these, you can relax—you're in the mainstream:

- Professional staff   70%
- Clerical/secretarial staff   16%
- External consultants   2%
- Materials, supplies, telephone 5%
- Data processing   3%
- Facilities   0%
- Travel   3%

Of course the estimates Alkin received varied a lot. Professional staff estimates, for example, ranged from 52% to 90% and data processing from nothing to 23%.

Most of Alkin's findings simply confirm your own common-sense observations. Costs are higher for evaluations of new and innovative programs than for the tried and true; clerical and secretarial expenses rise dramatically with the size of the total budget; travel costs more for field studies than nonfield studies.

But the data processing category is worth a second look. DP costs jump from 2% or less of the total budget on $4,000 evaluations to about 10% for $10,000 evaluations, then drop back to about 6% at the $25,000 level. As Alkin explains:

> "The total budget must be of a certain magnitude before it is either possible or worthwhile to use data processing services. However, data processing costs are relatively fixed; the initial outlay is high, but the incremental costs for added units are fairly low. Thus, the proportion of the budget allocated to data processing is smaller at the $25,000 level than at the $10,000 level."

In fact, the decision to analyze data by hand or by electronic means had such a striking effect on budget allocations that Alkin concluded the method of analysis should become a mediating variable in future studies of this kind.

At What Cost Testing?

Elsewhere in the same book James Catterall takes a preliminary swipe at ways to determine the costs of testing, another issue of critical interest to evaluators.

He begins with a simple list of the costs and benefits of testing. First, the usual costs for all tests: development, administration, analysis of results, and so on. Another list covers costs related to outside mandates, such as legislation, enforcement, compliance, remediation and legal fees.

Next come the benefits of testing, divided between information benefits, such as the ability to plan instruction, and noninformation benefits, such as incidental learning and student motivation.

Keeping this inventory of costs and benefits in mind, Catterall applies what he calls the cost-of-information paradigm, which "suggests that certain basic relationships hold between the amount of testing done and the benefits associated with such testing."

The principles of the paradigm are familiar to most evaluators. The first is the diminishing marginal utility of testing, which means that enough is enough, and more is not always better. The second says that the costs of testing depend on how much testing you do.

Here is a classroom example of the two principles at work, in Catterall's own words:

> "Consider the teacher's decision regarding what constitutes an appropriate amount of testing. On the one hand, testing confers benefits: in the form of information gained, which the teacher can then use to improve instruction, which in turn presumably will contribute to the educational development of the students; and perhaps in the form of incidental learning and increased motivation on the part of the students themselves. On the other hand, testing exacts a variety of costs: in the form of dollar costs for materials; in the form of opportunities lost for other learning activities. According to the model, then, added testing is a winning proposition up to a certain point; but after that, it becomes a less defensible proposition. Or, to put it another way, at some point the benefits gained from additional testing just equal its costs; after that point, the return begins to decline; when the benefits are less than the costs, one should not do any more testing."

Although he pursues this topic through another chapter on "Fundamental Issues in the Costing of Testing Programs," Catterall never quite tells us how to know when we have reached the point where testing is no longer worth the cost.

Perhaps we should feel reassured to know that he expects us to figure it out for ourselves, a task that will keep many of us gainfully employed in the years ahead.

References

Alkin, Marvin C., and Lewis C. Solmon, ed. <u>The Costs of Evaluation</u>. Beverly Hills, Calif.: Sage Publications.

This lesson is reprinted from the December 1984 issue of
<u>How To Evaluate Education Programs</u>.

NOTES

Lesson 14

How To Evaluate On A Shoestring

Some say the best evaluation is a true experiment with randomly selected groups and sophisticated statistical methods. Others believe the best evaluation requires an in-depth understanding of a program, that it relies on observations and interviews, and that it results in anecdotes and personal testimony.

Regardless of your approach, an evaluation is expensive. Ten percent of the program budget is what many evaluators say it takes to do a decent job. But what if you haven't got that kind of money? Is there an inexpensive way to conduct improvement (formative) evaluations of relatively small programs?

Here is a system, developed by the Commonwealth Fund of New York City, that won't break the budget. It will enable you to answer some basic questions like: Is this program living up to its promises? What can be done to improve it--or even save it? Are we right in supporting it?

Because the system calls for program staff to participate in evaluation, help can be provided quickly. You don't have to wait for the end of the program or until the evaluation report is published, when it may be too late.

Briefly, this evaluation review system requires you to survey program plans and accomplishments, listen to the staff and then ask independent reviewers to determine progress.

Start With A Survey Of The Program

Your first step is to design a questionnaire that will provide the information you and others need to make decisions about the program. At this stage, the information is only descriptive; judgments will come later.

The questionnaire has several purposes. They are to:

▶ Help developers and program staff see their program from the sponsor's perspective;

▶ Give reviewers essential information to use in appraising the merit or worth of the program; and

▶ Save reviewing time by eliminating extraneous details and distilling essential information.

There are two aspects to survey development. First, you have to have a clear idea of what data you really need, and second, you have to know something about the program you'll be reviewing. Among the issues you may want to consider is whether a program has achieved its purposes. You may want to know what its activities and methods are, and whether it's well run.

But you also need to consider the nature of the program. Is it designed to provide a service, such as school lunches or inservice training? Is it for research, like a needs assessment or a comparison of reading programs? The difference will probably affect the way you ask or phrase some of the questions. In a service program, you will probably be concerned with activities (Who's being served? How many?), while in a research program you may be more interested in methods (Is the sampling plan the best? Are the instruments reliable and valid?). Here's an example:

Sample Questionnaire For A Service Program

Name of program:_____

Persons completing this form:_____

Dates of program:_____

Funding level:_____

Principal investigator
or project director:_____

1. Is the program achieving its purposes and objectives?

   These are the intended benefits. Many service programs are intended to change or improve health, social or education services by paying attention to:

   ■ The individuals or groups who receive them (Who has been served? How have knowledge, attitudes, or behavior changed?)
   ■ Costs (Have costs been reduced or allocated more efficiently or fairly?)
   ■ Structure (Are services organized and administered so that they are accessible? Comprehensive? Coordinated?)

   Programs also may have as their purpose the testing of hypotheses, answering questions about effectiveness or discovering the best way to perform services.

2. What activities are taking place?

   The activities are what the program is doing to bring about beneficial changes. Examples might be setting up an advisory panel; training data collectors; conducting a survey; reorganizing staff; providing financial support.

3. What are the program's major accomplishments so far?

   These may include, for example:

   ■ Establishing or validating an innovative treatment;
   ■ Expanding existing services;
   ■ Developing or using new methods or technology;
   ■ Helping a large number or a special group of individuals;
   ■ Making presentations at public or professional meetings.

4. How is the program being managed?

   This refers primarily to the stability of leadership and the efficiency of the project. For example:

   ■ Have the same people been in charge of the project since the beginning? Is staff turnover a problem?
   ■ Are records and accounts in order and up to date?

If you are evaluating a research program rather than a service program, you might want to rephrase some of the questions, or ask different ones. For example:

---

1. Is the program achieving its purposes and objectives?

   These are the intended outcomes. Some examples of research purposes are to:
   - Test hypotheses or answer research questions;
   - Develop and validate new research methods and technology;
   - Develop and validate new programs, treatments or organizations.

2. What methods are used to achieve program objectives?

   Methods might include:
   - *Research design:* How was the environment changed or variables manipulated so that the observed effects could be reliably linked to the program?
   - *Sampling:* How were individuals, groups, or units selected?
   - *Observation/measurement:* How were data collected? Are measurements reliable? Valid?

Searching For Answers In Program Documents

Now that you have a questionnaire on which to base your survey, you should begin reviewing program documents. Here are examples of documents you might want to take a look at:

▶ The contract or letter of understanding with the sponsor;

▶ Any progress reports or data on activities and participants;

▶ Program products such as curriculum materials, statements of objectives, data collection instruments, and so on; and

▶ Internal memoranda describing such things as staff, organization, or schedules.

After you have studied the documents, fill out a questionnaire. Remember to keep the information descriptive. Don't pass judgment until program officials have a chance to verify the accuracy of your information and explain their progress personally.

This leads to the next step, which is to get reaction from the staff. Ask them to review the completed questionnaire to be sure you haven't omitted anything they consider important. Give the people in charge a week or two to look it over and make comments, corrections, or additions. This is the time to clear up any mistakes or misinterpretations.

At the end of the allotted time, reconcile your findings with those of the project staff. If there are conflicts, be sure to include both sides of the story on the final questionnaire.

The following example shows a completed questionnaire for a program that is supposed to give disadvantaged high schoolers a chance to get summer jobs in the private sector. The cast of participants includes four city high schools, 10 private companies (the phone company, banks, department stores, a camera shop), a local college and a philanthropic foundation.

The evaluator's comments are in regular type; the project staff's are in italics. To save space, we deleted the explanation and examples following each question, but these should be a standard part of the questionnaire form.

Completed Service Program Questionnaire

Name of program: **Career Explorations: A Summer And Career Program For Youth**

Persons completing this form: **Arlene Fink and Jacqueline Kosecoff**

Dates of program: **6/8/82 — 12/31/82**

Funding level: **$199,460**

Principal investigator or project director: **Roberta Samuels, Ed.D., and Robert Moore, M.A.**

1. Is the program achieving its purpose and objectives?

* * *

PLACE YOUR RESPONSE HERE:

This program is a pilot study to determine if an academic institution, private enterprise, and private philanthropy can provide interesting jobs and work experience for boys and girls from inner-city schools. Specifically, Linn College, the Post Foundation and a number of private profit-making and nonprofit firms and agencies are collaborating to support a program of over 200 high school juniors. The New York Community Trust also provided some assistance.

The program offers: weekly career seminars at Linn; job-site supervision by members or friends of the Coalition of Women ("mentors") working at the participating companies; overall supervision by 10 field supervisors drawn from Linn College; and clearly defined student rights and responsibilities. An independent evaluation of the program itself is being conducted by Pamela Robbins of the sociology department at Linn.

Preliminary findings of that evaluation indicate:

- 93 percent of the 207 students who began the program are still in it;
- Field supervisors rate at least half the students highly competent;
- Students give their jobs an overall score of 3.3 on a 4-point scale;
- Mentors are rated excellent by 68 percent of the students, with an average rating of 3.6; and
- Field supervisors are rated excellent by 76 percent of students.

The Robbins evaluation says: "Judging from the results of the evaluation, the program appears to be well run and successful in meeting its goals by providing city teen-agers with interesting summer jobs and raising their career aspirations."

In our view, several questions of future interest remain unanswered. We would like to know, for example, what "model" of cooperation between schools, colleges, private sector and foundation was most effective. No documents describe the relationship between groups. Is it formal, or does success depend on the strong leadership of this particular project's organizers and staff? The question of how to enlist the support of the private sector also is not answered.

Finally, the timetable for the grant seems so short that we cannot imagine how to determine the effect of the program on students' career choices, which was one of the stated goals.

2. What activities took place?

* * *

PLACE YOUR RESPONSE HERE:

The most successful activity appears to be the use of field supervisors who are described as helpful, readily available, and good at conveying program rules.

The Coalition of Women was crucial in helping us to place students.

3. What were the program's main accomplishments?

* * *

PLACE YOUR RESPONSE HERE:

The main accomplishment has been to provide provisional confirmation that an academic institution and the private sector can work together effectively to offer inner-city youth interesting summer jobs.

Another important accomplishment was to get the word to inner-city kids that summer jobs are possible. We are including a list of 20 students who have already inquired about the program for next summer.

4. How has the program been managed?

* * *

PLACE YOUR RESPONSE HERE:

The staff was stable and record-keeping was adequate.

5. What attempts have been made to let the public and others know about the program?

* * *

PLACE YOUR RESPONSE HERE:

No information.

One article about our efforts has already appeared in our local paper.

6. What problems has the program encountered?

* * *

PLACE YOUR RESPONSE HERE:

Most of the problems seem to be due to the lack of start-up time. The entire program was organized between May 17 and July 2. By the time students and businesses were contacted in June, summer commitments had already been made. Short notice also made it difficult to get speakers for the weekly career seminars.

The students are having some difficulties. Since they have no identification cards, for example, some are having trouble cashing checks.

How To Use A Review Panel

Choose up to five reviewer/evaluators and explain that their job is to reach some agreement about program progress. Before the meeting give them the completed questionnaire and a brief summary (say three typewritten pages) of the original program plans.

Using the questionnaire as a starting point, have the program developers or staff personally describe their achievements. Allow a certain amount of time for the presentation, leaving time for discussion. Scheduling depends on how long the panel can spend on this review.

After the program staff make their presentation, have them leave the room. Then ask the reviewer/evaluators to rate the merits of the program.

It helps to provide them with a rating sheet with a brief definition of each rating category. Here's how a rating form for a service program might look:

PROGRAM RATING FORM

Category	A	B	C	D	F	NA	Comments
Objectives and Purposes How well is the program achieving its objectives and purposes?							
Activities How carefully are the activities chosen and carried out?							
Accomplishments How significant are the program's accomplishments so far?							
Management How good is program management?							
Dissemination How well is the staff disseminating information about the program?							
General Rating How would you rate the overall progress and merit of the program?							

Rating Scale:
A = Excellent (Meeting the highest standards. Reliable and valid methods and outcomes.)
B = Good (High level of performance, although some areas need improvement.)
C = Average (Fair level of performance. Modifications needed.)
D = Poor (Not achieving at a satisfactory level. Outcomes may be questionable.)
F = Fail (Unsatisfactory. Unreliable. Invalid.)
NA = Not applicable.

There are several ways to turn the ratings form into a useful indicator of progress. One is to have each panelist complete the form and for you to average the ratings. Letter ratings can be placed on a numerical scale, from A = 4 to F = 0. Add the number ratings and divide by the number of reviewers to come up with an average score for program progress.

Another way you may be able to reach a consensus is by asking one person to act as leader of the group. The leader assigns a rating for each category, and the other members of the panel agree or disagree with the leader's assessment. In case of disagreement, be sure to include a "minority report."

Give sponsors, program developers, and staff the results of the review as soon as possible, while there is time to improve program performance. Always point out strengths as well as weaknesses.

This kind of evaluation is not as rigorous as most of us would like, but it has several advantages. It's fast, inexpensive, and generally recognized as fair by sponsors and program people alike.

This lesson is reprinted from the June 1983 issue of
<u>How To Evaluate Education Programs</u>.

Here is an extra questionnaire sample for you to cut out and use.

Sample Questionnaire For A Service Program

Name of program:_____

Persons completing this form:_____

Dates of program:_____

Funding level:_____

Principal investigator
or project director:_____

1. Is the program achieving its purposes and objectives?

2. What activities are taking place?

3. What are the program's major accomplishments so far?

4. How is the program being managed?

Here is an extra program rating form for you to cut out and use.

PROGRAM RATING FORM

Category	A	B	C	D	F	NA	Comments
Objectives and Purposes How well is the program achieving its objectives and purposes?							
Activities How carefully are the activities chosen and carried out?							
Accomplishments How significant are the program's accomplishments so far?							
Management How good is program management?							
Dissemination How well is the staff disseminating information about the program?							
General Rating How would you rate the overall progress and merit of the program?							

Rating Scale:
A = Excellent (Meeting the highest standards. Reliable and valid methods and outcomes.)
B = Good (High level of performance, although some areas need improvement.)
C = Average (Fair level of performance. Modifications needed.)
D = Poor (Not achieving at a satisfactory level. Outcomes may be questionable.)
F = Fail (Unsatisfactory. Unreliable. Invalid.)
NA = Not applicable.

NOTES

Lesson 15

How To Avoid Common Evaluation Hazards

A research team looking for effective compensatory math and reading programs once waded through 2,000 projects without finding a single evaluation that provided acceptable evidence of success or failure. In every case, problems in conducting and reporting the evaluations rendered the results inconclusive.

What were the problems those investigators encountered in their search? They fell roughly into 12 "common hazards," as they explained later in A Practical Guide To Measuring Project Impact On Student Achievement, by Donald P. Horst, G. Kasten Tallmadge and Christine T. Wood of the RMC Research Corp.

Evaluation is not as haphazard as it was back in the 1970s, when that search took place. Now we can point to standards set by groups like the Joint Dissemination Review Panel and the Joint Committee on Standards for Educational Evaluation. Many test publishers have improved their procedures, as well.

But have we stamped out the 12 common hazards that troubled our predecessors? You be the judge. Remember, committing just one of these sins is enough to invalidate an otherwise sound evaluation.

Hazard #1: Using Grade-Equivalent Scores

Grade equivalent scores are insensitive measures that sometimes distort the picture of a project's impact. What's wrong with using grade equivalents? They have three serious problems.

First, the concept of a "grade-equivalent" score is misleading. If a fifth grader gets a grade-equivalent score of seven on a math test, for example, it doesn't mean he knows seventh-grade math. It's closer to say that he can do fifth-grade math as well as an average seventh grader can do fifth-grade math. Grade equivalents, as in this case, are usually just statistical projections. They can't tell us how seventh graders would have actually scored if they had taken the fifth-grade test.

Second, grade-equivalent scores don't fit into an equal interval scale. In other words, a grade-equivalent score of two is not "half" of a score of four. This means "average" grade-equivalent scores are not consistent with averages computed from most other scores and can't be interpreted.

Finally, there's the way the normative data for most commercial tests are collected. This is during one short interval of the school year, often in February or March. To establish norms for fall and spring, a smooth survey is drawn connecting the points, which represent actual data.

But learning doesn't progress uniformly over the calendar year. Summer takes its toll on student achievement, making grade-equivalent scores too low in the fall and too high in the spring. Fall to spring gains sometimes look too good to be true ... because they are.

How can you avoid the grade-equivalent hazard? Go ahead and use standardized tests, but convert raw scores to standard scores instead of grade-equivalent scores before computing summary statistics. Next, convert mean pretest and posttest standard scores to their percentile equivalents.

Finally, if you administered the tests at appropriate times (see Hazard #3), you can compare group pretest-to-posttest gains with expected gains derived from national norms.

Hazard #2: Using Gain Scores

Gain scores are sometimes used to adjust for initial differences between treatment and comparison groups in experimental designs. This is a bad practice that does more harm than good.

The most commonly used gain score is the "raw" gain score, which is simply the posttest score minus the pretest score. (The term "raw" actually refers to the gain, not the score.)

If differences between treatment and comparison groups are random (as in random samples from a single population), then raw gain scores overcorrect for pretest differences by excessively inflating the posttest performance measure of the initially inferior group. Use analysis of covariance, instead, to make the adjustment for random pretreatment differences.

If differences between treatment and comparison groups are real, no amount of statistical juggling will fix it.

How can you avoid the gain score hazard? Never use them! If pretest scores are equal for treatment and comparison groups, you don't need to make any adjustment. If differences are from random sampling fluctuations, use covariance analysis. If the differences are real and the groups are not comparable, don't use a comparison-group model. Try some other evaluation design instead.

Hazard #3: Using Norm-Group Comparisons With Inappropriate Test Dates

Don't make norm-referenced comparisons unless you administer tests on dates that correspond to those when the normative data were collected.

Most publishers provide norms for fall, winter and spring, even though they collect the data only once or twice a year. To project norms, they generally assume students learn evenly for each month of the nine months of school. Then they add another month's gain for the three summer months.

Using norms that have been created this way can seriously distort the results of instructional programs.

How can you avoid this hazard? In the words of Horst and his RMC colleagues:

"It is absolutely essential to test children in the treatment condition within a few weeks of the dates on which the norm groups were tested. Tests which provide normative data for only one point in the year should not be used for norm-referenced evaluation of fall-to-spring gains.

"Instead, it is better to select a test with normative data in both fall and spring even though the choice of tests is then limited. Basically, it is never advisable to extrapolate or interpolate very far from observed normative data."

Hazard #4: Using The Wrong Levels Of Tests

If almost everyone is getting the right answers, or if hardly anyone is, you are using the wrong level of test for that group. The results will be unreliable and invalid. Ideally, pupils should land somewhere in the middle of the possible range of scores.

Standardized achievement tests are divided into several levels. Each level is an individual test suitable for only two or three grades. If your project is aimed at slow or fast learners, the test level for their grade is likely to be too hard (many will land on the test "floor") or too easy (many will hit the test "ceiling"). Floor and ceiling effects can also distort evaluations that use criterion-reference tests.

How can you avoid this hazard? Select test levels that match your students' achievement levels, not their grade in school. Choosing one level above or below that recommended for a particular grade is usually enough to avoid floor and ceiling effects.

When you use test levels that are not the ones recommended for a particular grade, you may be unable to find corresponding norms tables in the test manual. Too bad, because you certainly don't want to make comparisons with children at a different grade level. A sixth grader should be assessed by sixth-grade norms even if he took a fourth-grade test.

Fortunately, most big test publishers provide overlapping grade-level coverage, making it possible to predict quite accurately from a pupil's score on one test level how he would have scored on the next higher or lower level.

No matter what test level you choose, always use the same level for both pretest and posttest (see Hazard #10).

Hazard #5: Not Having Pretest And Posttest Scores For Each Participant

When analyzing project impact, include only the participants with both pretest and posttest scores. Later, when you interpret the data, it's a good idea to note the characteristics of pupils who dropped out, entered late, or graduated.

In most projects, the students who show up for the posttest are not exactly the same ones who took the pretest. Dropouts and new students change the composition of the group during the school year. This means that pretest and posttest mean scores are not strictly comparable. Dropouts, for example, are often among the slowest students. By eliminating their low scores from the posttest, you could get a rosier assessment of progress than the project deserves.

It may work the other way if the program returns successful students to their regular classrooms. Eliminate their posttest scores and you may get a gloomier picture than you should.

The RMC researchers frequently encountered evaluation reports that included posttest scores for fewer than half of the program participants. They considered such reports meaningless.

Can you avoid this hazard? Yes. You can't stop students from dropping out or entering a project after it has begun, but you can keep them out of the data base from which you draw conclusions about project impact. Use data only on students who have both pretest and posttest scores.

But dropouts are important. Examine their pretest score distribution to see if it differs from that of the nondropouts. If you have a lot of dropouts, try to find out why. Did they succeed and go on to better things, or did they fail and give up in despair? Are there systematic differences between dropouts and those who remained? These are crucial questions for program evaluation.

Hazard #6: Using Noncomparable Treatment And Comparison Groups

Students in a special program may do better or worse than comparison groups simply because they were different to start with. In experimental designs, treatment and comparison groups must be comparable in all significant respects before treatment begins. This includes variables like pretest scores, age, sex, socioeconomic status, racial and ethnic composition, and school size and setting. Beware of using volunteers in a special program and assigning the rest to a comparison group. Subtle differences like this are often overlooked.

Be even more careful when you are using norm-based comparisons. Volunteering and some other selection methods can result in a treatment group quite different from the students in the norm group who had comparable pretest scores.

Can you avoid this hazard? The surest way is to assign treatment and comparison groups on a random basis, or at least in a way that is random in effect. (See Hazard #2 for other suggestions closely related to this problem.)

Hazard #7: Selecting Participants By Their Pretest Scores

If you select students for a project because they scored high or low on some test, and then you use those scores as pretest measures, it invalidates any norm-referenced evaluation.

The same thing is true for experimental designs unless you select the comparison-group students in exactly the same way. Most evaluators are aware of this problem, but it still pops up from time to time.

We know that when low-scoring students are retested on the same or a comparable test, they will score higher on the average, while an initially high-scoring group will score lower. This is called statistical regression. It makes low scores appear to learn more from a special program than they actually do, and it obscures gains for high-scoring students.

How can you avoid this hazard? It is safer not to use the pretest to select project participants. Corrections for regression effect are possible in theory, but you usually don't have the data necessary to do it.

Or you can avoid the problems by using a special regression model in your evaluation design that specifically calls for selecting participants on the basis of pretest performance.

Hazard #8: Assembling A Comparison Group After Selecting Project Participants

The common practice of selecting students for the treatment, then trying to find a nontreatment student to match each treatment student is a serious evaluation error.

Suppose you set up a project for low achievers in a disadvantaged school, and then construct a "matching" group made up of children with equally low pretest scores from other schools. The comparison students are likely to be farther below the means of their own schools than the treatment children, so their posttest scores would show a greater regression toward the mean. This inflates the apparent gains of the comparison group and might obscure a real project impact.

This is how to avoid this hazard. Start with a large group of students, all eligible for the project. Divide the group into matched pairs based on test scores, ethnic background, and so forth, so that the members of each pair are as much alike as possible. Then use some random procedure such as flipping a coin to decide which one of each pair goes into treatment and which into the comparison group.

If you can't do it this way, select another model that doesn't require matched groups.

Hazard #9: Administering Or Scoring Tests Carelessly

For most evaluation models, it's imperative to test treatment and comparison groups in exactly the same way. Norm-referenced models also require that you follow exactly the procedures outlined by test publishers.

If there are differences in the ways students are tested, or differences in the procedures, conditions and scoring at pretest and posttest times, you can't trust the results to accurately reflect project impact. No amount of careful statistical analysis after the fact can overcome these problems.

How can you avoid this hazard? Using trained personnel cuts the risk of careless mistakes such as failing to get the right name on each answer sheet, using the wrong answer key, or copying incorrect scores onto data sheets.

In testing treatment and comparison groups, always use identical procedures. Sometimes it is even possible to use the same tester for both groups.

In making norm-group comparisons, follow the test instructions exactly.

To make sure the pretest and posttest situations are comparable, it might help to have an external evaluator administer the tests, or have teachers exchange classrooms to test and score each other's students. This avoids the problem of a few teachers who are so eager to show achievement gains that they enforce time limits more strictly on the pretest than the posttest, or offer helpful hints on the posttest.

Hazard #10: Assuming That Gains Are Due To The Treatment

Before you attribute achievement gains to the project, examine the plausibility of other explanations.

Sometimes participants do well simply because they're getting special treatment. Changes in school programs or teachers, or participation in another program at the same time could also lead to ambiguous results.

To avoid this hazard, just don't leap to conclusions. If you find a significant cognitive achievement gain when you evaluate a program, look for other explanations. Examine each rival hypothesis and try to eliminate it as a likely reason for the gain.

If you evaluate the same program in later years, you may be able to control or eliminate these alternative explanations.

Hazard #11: Using Noncomparable Pretest And Posttest

Always try to use the same _level_ of the same _test_ for both pretesting and posttesting. Sometimes tests are changed on a districtwide basis during the evaluation period, for reasons beyond your control. Even if you can't do anything about it, you should recognize that it may severely limit the usefulness of your evaluation.

This is not a critical problem in a comparison-group design, but it is a major one for norm-referenced designs. There's just no way to compare pretest scores on one test with posttest scores on a completely different test. Each test is normed on a different group, which means you would be using one comparison group for the pretest and another comparison group for the posttest.

How can you avoid this hazard? The only way to be sure with norm-referenced evaluations is to administer the same level of the same test on both occasions. In comparison-group designs, it may be okay to switch from one standardized a test to another if they are similar and meet requirements for validity and reliability. This may lower the precision of the evaluation, since pretest-posttest correlations will not be as high as when you use the same test.

Hazard #12: Using Questionable Formulas To Estimate Posttest Scores

Occasionally evaluators will use a theoretical model or formula to calculate "expected" posttest scores from IQ or other pretest scores. If students do better than the calculated expectation, the project is considered a success.

Estimated posttest scores are often based on average grade-equivalent scores and suffer from all the problems explained in Hazard #1. Others use IQ scores to calculate expected gains. IQ tests have some practical uses, but they are not the best predictors of specific school skills.

You can avoid this hazard by using national norms to estimate posttest scores in norm-referenced models. When you have comparison groups, use actual posttest scores (or a regression equation estimating posttest scores) to evaluate treatment effects.

This lesson is reprinted from the July 1983 issue of
How To Evaluate Education Programs.

NOTES

Evaluation Formulas

Chi Square Formula (*see Lesson 3, page 23*):

$$X^2 = \sum_{i=1}^{n} \frac{(o_i - t_i)^2}{t_i}$$

where: n = number of categories

o_i = obtained or empirical frequency for the ith category

t_i = theoretical or expected frequency for the ith category

Standard Deviation Formula (*see Lesson 7, page 61*):

$$S^2 = \frac{\sum (x - \bar{x})^2}{N}$$

where: S^2 = variance

$\sum$ = "the sum of"

x = the single unit whose standard deviation from the norm is to be determined

$\bar{x}$ = the mean of all units used to determine the norm

N = the total of all units used to determine the norm

Relationship of a Normal Curve to the Standard Normal Curve (*see Lesson 7, page 61*)

$$x = \mu + z\sigma \quad \text{or} \quad z = \frac{x - \mu}{\sigma}$$

where: x = a point on the horizontal axis of a normal curve

μ = mean value of the normal curve

σ = standard deviation of the normal curve

z = the point on the standard normal curve to which x corresponds

Null Hypothesis (*see Lesson 8, page 71*):

$$H_o: \bar{X}_A = \bar{X}_B$$

where: H_o = the null hypothesis of no difference between groups

$\bar{X}_A$ = the mean value of group A

$\bar{X}^B$ = the mean value of group B

Evaluation Formulas

Binomial Distribution Formula (*see Lesson 10, page 87*):

$$\binom{N}{x} \left(\frac{1}{2}\right)^N = \frac{N!}{x!(N-x)!} \left(\frac{1}{2}\right)^N$$

where: N = the number of times the value of group A is greater than the value of group B (+) plus the number of times the value of group A is less than the value of group B (−)

x = the number of times the value of group A is less than the value of group B

! = the factorial product of the designated number (e.g., if x = 4, then x! = 4 x 3 x 2 x 1)

NOTES

NOTES

NOTES

NOTES

TAKE YOUR PICK

OF THE SPECIALIZED NEWSLETTERS AND REPORTS THAT PRECISELY MEET YOUR EDUCATION INFORMATION NEEDS...

Education Daily
Six pages daily. $429.95 per year/$245.95 for six months.

Up-to-the-minute reports on national, state and local events pertinent to top-level educators. Includes news from Congress, the Education Department and the courts—as well as the weekly Legislative Update and the weekly supplement on available funding, **Money Alert**.

Higher Education Daily
Six pages daily. $459.95 per year/$254.95 for six months.

Fast, reliable news about federal, state and local activity affecting colleges and universities. Covers developments in the federal bureaucracy, Congress, the courts and associations. Regularly reports on research policy and student aid news. Includes the weekly Legislative Update.

Report on Education Research
Ten pages biweekly. $169.95 per year.

News of research findings, research programs, funding and policy. Regularly covers the Education Department and the education labs and centers. Focuses on testing and evaluation, education reforms and related topics of interest to administrators and researchers.

Nation's Schools Report
Eight pages—22 issues. $128.95 per year.

Common sense reports on what education administrators around the country are doing to pare costs and solve tangled administrative and financial problems. Includes reports on legal decisions, national news, education news, resources and more.

Education Computer News
Ten pages biweekly. $176.95 per year.

Concise reports for educators and administrators who need dependable, independent news on education technology from microcomputers to video disks to fiber optics. Covers trends, new products, legislation, teacher training, research, and state and local news.

Report on Education of the Disadvantaged
Ten pages biweekly. $178.95 per year.

Washington news affecting Chapter 1, bilingual education, child nutrition programs, programs for migrant children and related topics of special interest. Keeps subscribers informed on program or funding changes.

School Law News
Ten pages biweekly. $177.95 per year.

Keeps school administrators and legal advisers informed of legal decisions, pending court cases and critical issues that affect schools. Covers the federal judiciary, the Supreme Court, state courts, the federal bureaucracy and developments on Capitol Hill.

Student Aid News
Ten pages biweekly. $189.95 per year.

Latest news on federal programs affecting financial aid to postsecondary students, including Guaranteed Student Loans, Pell Grants, National Direct Student Loans, Auxiliary Loans to Assist Students, Health Professions Student Loans and non-federal loan programs. Regular coverage of Congress, the Education Department and Sallie Mae.

Equal Opportunity in Higher Education
Ten pages biweekly. $171.95 per year.

Reports on all action taken in connection with claims of race, sex and handicap bias in America's postsecondary institutions. Covers federal and state court cases, legislation, regulations on affirmative action and anti-bias law compliance, and survey and research results.

How to Evaluate Education Programs
Eight pages monthly. $119.95 per year.

Workable solutions to the most often encountered problems of education program evaluation. Covers data collecting, needs assessment and minimum competency standards. Gives fast, easy-to-understand answers to help educators master program evaluation techniques.

Education of the Handicapped
Ten pages biweekly. $180.95 per year.

The most current information available about federal legislation, regulations, programs and funding for educating handicapped children. Covers federal and state litigation under the Education for All Handicapped Children Act and other relevant laws. Looks at innovations and research in the field.

College Marketing Alert
Ten pages biweekly. $274.95 per year.

Valuable and concise marketing information to help today's admissions, development, public relations and student aid professionals boost enrollments and funds. Packed with actual strategies that have worked well for others, covering the areas of advertising, recruiting and retention, development and fundraising, and market research.

SPECIAL REPORTS FROM CAPITOL PUBLICATIONS' EDUCATION RESEARCH GROUP

The Child Abuse Crisis: Impact on the Schools
120 pages. $35.

Covers what states and districts are doing to detect and eliminate child abuse, the benefits and problems with the new screening laws and the legal responsibilities of reporting child abuse cases. Extensive statistical and resource listings.

P.L. 94-142: Impact on the Schools
365 pages. $55.

A provocative look at one of the most far-reaching pieces of federal education legislation ever, the report includes results of an exclusive survey of school administrators nationwide, complete text of the Education of the Handicapped Act and regulations, a guide to lawsuits, extensive telephone directories and more.

Education Directory: A Guide to Decision-Makers in the Federal Government, the States and Education Associations
85 pages. $45.

The most comprehensive listing available anywhere of top education administrators nationwide. Includes the Education Department and other federal agencies, chief state school officers, state education committee chairmen and more.

Inside the Education Department: An Office-by-Office Review
80 pages. $24.95.

From Education Secretary William Bennett to the program officers responsible for federal education funding, this report profiles the major divisions of the multibillion dollar Education Department. Included are extensive program descriptions and telephone numbers.

AIDS: Impact on the Schools
288 pages. $65.

Tackles the hard questions behind the AIDS-in-the-schools controversy and gives you easy-to-understand explanations of the disease itself. Extensive appendices include the text of Centers for Disease Control guidelines on AIDS for both students and employees, samples of state and local guidelines on AIDS in the schools, groups and associations around the country you can call for the latest facts, and an extensive glossary of AIDS-related terms.

Education Regulations Library
Eight volumes, sold separately or as a set.

America's only customized reference library of federal education rules and laws is an eight-volume set, divided by subject and containing the full text of all regulations and laws governing education programs. A one-year subscription to **Education Regulations Update**, a monthly newsletter on regulatory changes, is included in the purchase of one or more volumes.

☐ *Volume I: General Education Provisions* ($59 when purchased as companion volume to any other book/$118 when purchased separately)
☐ *Volume II: Elementary and Secondary Education* $195
☐ *Volume III: Special Education* $175
☐ *Volume IV: Vocational Education and Job Training* $159
☐ *Volume V: Student Aid/Postsecondary Education* $197
☐ *Volume VI: Education Research* $99
☐ *Volume VII: Child Nutrition* $179
☐ *Volume VIII: Education Laws* $229
  ☐ *Complete Eight-Volume Set* $969 (a 25% savings)

Also available from the Education Research Group:
A complete document retrieval service. For a master list of documents available, or for personalized document retrieval services, contact Sharon Larrimer, document retrieval coordinator, at (703) 528-1100.

Education Research Group, Capitol Publications, Inc., 1101 King Street, P.O. Box 1453, Alexandria, VA 22313-2053

THE EDUCATION EVALUATOR'S WORKBOOK:
How To Assess Education Programs

✓ **YES,** I need to learn how to evaluate my programs effectively and efficiently. Please send me _____ copies of **The Education Evaluator's Workbook: How to Assess Education Programs** today at $_____ per copy. (Check table below for correct price.)

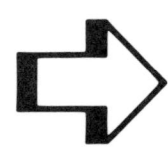

Name/Title_____

Organization_____

Street Address_____

City/State/Zip_____

For faster service, call TOLL FREE 1-800-327-7204
Monday-Friday, 9-5 EST. In Virginia, call collect (703) 739-6500.

EDUCATION RESEARCH GROUP
Capitol Publications, Inc., 1101 King Street, P.O. Box 1453, Alexandria, VA 22313-2053

☐ Check enclosed (Payable to Capitol Publications, Inc.)
☐ Bill me/my organization _____
　Purchase order number
☐ Charge ☐ VISA ☐ MasterCard ☐ American Express

Account # _____ Expiration date _____

Signature (required for billing and credit orders) _____

No. of Copies	Price
1-5	$37.95
6-10	34.00
11-25	30.00
26 +	23.00

THE EDUCATION EVALUATOR'S WORKBOOK:
How To Assess Education Programs

✓ **YES,** I need to learn how to evaluate my programs effectively and efficiently. Please send me _____ copies of **The Education Evaluator's Workbook: How to Assess Education Programs** today at $_____ per copy. (Check table below for correct price.)

Name/Title_____

Organization_____

Street Address_____

City/State/Zip_____

For faster service, call TOLL FREE 1-800-327-7204
Monday-Friday, 9-5 EST. In Virginia, call collect (703) 739-6500.

EDUCATION RESEARCH GROUP
Capitol Publications, Inc., 1101 King Street, P.O. Box 1453, Alexandria, VA 22313-2053

☐ Check enclosed (Payable to Capitol Publications, Inc.)
☐ Bill me/my organization _____
　Purchase order number
☐ Charge ☐ VISA ☐ MasterCard ☐ American Express

Account # _____ Expiration date _____

Signature (required for billing and credit orders) _____

No. of Copies	Price
1-5	$37.95
6-10	34.00
11-25	30.00
26 +	23.00

THE EDUCATION EVALUATOR'S WORKBOOK:
How To Assess Education Programs

✓ **YES,** I need to learn how to evaluate my programs effectively and efficiently. Please send me _____ copies of **The Education Evaluator's Workbook: How to Assess Education Programs** today at $_____ per copy. (Check table below for correct price.)

Name/Title_____

Organization_____

Street Address_____

City/State/Zip_____

For faster service, call TOLL FREE 1-800-327-7204
Monday-Friday, 9-5 EST. In Virginia, call collect (703) 739-6500.

EDUCATION RESEARCH GROUP
Capitol Publications, Inc., 1101 King Street, P.O. Box 1453, Alexandria, VA 22313-2053

☐ Check enclosed (Payable to Capitol Publications, Inc.)
☐ Bill me/my organization _____
　Purchase order number
☐ Charge ☐ VISA ☐ MasterCard ☐ American Express

Account # _____ Expiration date _____

Signature (required for billing and credit orders) _____

No. of Copies	Price
1-5	$37.95
6-10	34.00
11-25	30.00
26 +	23.00

BUSINESS REPLY MAIL
FIRST CLASS   PERMIT NO. 7474   ALEXANDRIA, VIRGINIA

POSTAGE WILL BE PAID BY ADDRESSEE

Capitol Publications, Inc.
BUSINESS & EDUCATION DIVISION
P.O. Box 1453
Alexandria, VA 22313-9990

No postage necessary if mailed in the United States

BUSINESS REPLY MAIL
FIRST CLASS   PERMIT NO. 7474   ALEXANDRIA, VIRGINIA

POSTAGE WILL BE PAID BY ADDRESSEE

Capitol Publications, Inc.
BUSINESS & EDUCATION DIVISION
P.O. Box 1453
Alexandria, VA 22313-9990

No postage necessary if mailed in the United States

BUSINESS REPLY MAIL
FIRST CLASS   PERMIT NO. 7474   ALEXANDRIA, VIRGINIA

POSTAGE WILL BE PAID BY ADDRESSEE

Capitol Publications, Inc.
BUSINESS & EDUCATION DIVISION
P.O. Box 1453
Alexandria, VA 22313-9990

No postage necessary if mailed in the United States